Foreword by Carl E. Brown, Jr. - State/Executive Director,
District of Columbia Small Business Development Center

CASHFLOW
CONTENT

Turn What You Know Into What You're Known For
and Become the Obvious Choice

MARK IMPERIAL

To business owners…the real engine of the world. The ones who take risks, create value, solve problems, and keep everything moving while everyone else is still "thinking about it."

I see you. I respect you. And I built this book for you so you can memorialize your magic and become "known-for" it.

To my peers, mentors, and fellow marketing and branding nerds, thank you for sharpening the thinking, challenging the ideas, and raising the standard.

To Gemma, Jomie, Jose, Tyler, Parker, and my team: you are proof that it takes a village to be this awesome.

And to Shannon, my brilliant editor and better half, without you, this book would either be twice as long… or make me look like an absolute idiot.

Probably both.

Access the Book Resources

Download all companion resources at:
www.cashflowcontentbook.com/resources

You can also scan the QR code below.

"I've known Mark Imperial for about 12 years, and if there's one thing I can tell you, it's this: Mark is the Voice of Authority. Not because he claims to be, because he earned it. Years of experience in radio and working closely with business owners taught him something most people never figure out. How to pull the true value out of the people he works with. He has this rare ability to sit across from someone, draw out the brilliance they didn't even know they were sitting on, wrap it up in easily digestible nuggets, and put a spotlight on what they can share with the world.

Cashflow Content is Mark in a book. It's the same clarity, the same no-nonsense thinking, and the same gift for cutting through the noise that I've watched him deliver for over a decade. If you've ever felt like what you know far exceeds what people know you for, this book will show you exactly how to close that gap. Mark doesn't just talk about turning expertise into authority. He hands you the blueprint."

Jack Mize
Author and Media Marketing Strategist
JackMize.com

"One of the biggest problems online is that it's hard to know which online marketers you can trust. Most don't have the client in mind and aren't running a long-term strategy, just jumping to whatever tactic works for the next few weeks.

Not only is Mark Imperial the opposite of that, but he's also working to uplift the industry, where especially given the economy, businesses need to market harder than ever to survive. *Cashflow Content* is Mark's help flow to businesses that don't know who to trust, but know they need to market.

*If you are someone who is looking to get the right visibility to scale your business and survive in an economy that's left just about everyone concerned about the future, then **Cashflow Content** is a book you need to have."*

Jeremy Ryan Slate
Founder, The Roman Pattern
www.jeremyryanslate.com

If you're looking for just another book about "content" with the same old, worn-out, sounds-good-but-doesn't-actually-work advice, there are a bazillion dime-a-dozen, run-of-the-mill so-called "experts" out there who will all tell you the same thing.

But this book is different. Mark Imperial is the real deal. And he tells you how it really is.

In this masterpiece, Mark shares with you how he has built several multi-million dollar brands, how he's become trusted and respected by an ever-growing audience, and how he's helped thousands of other business owners do the same.

Get ready to pay attention, to learn the truth about how creating the right content in the right way will work to build your business, and most of all to take action on what you are about to discover that will change your perspective, and your bank account, forever.

Steve Sipress
Founder and CEO of Successful Selling Systems

"As a business owner, you have a unique vision and the power to make a real difference, but too often, incredible talent remains trapped in marketing silence. To truly add value and inspire change, you must shift your business from obscurity into absolute significance. Mark Imperial understands this journey deeply and brings a remarkably keen approach to business development. He specializes in taking complex branding strategies and making them incredibly clear and concise for busy entrepreneurs. Mark gives you the practical tools to cut through the market noise so your target audience finally hears your authentic voice.

If you are ready to elevate your brand, reading his book, **Cashflow Content**, is an absolute must. Mark is an expert in transforming your core message into something deeply meaningful and instantly memorable to the exact people you are called to serve. When you master his blueprint for memorable communication, that genuine connection naturally leads to monetization and sustained business growth. This book will equip and energize you to stop being the best-kept secret in your industry and start claiming your destiny as a recognized authority."

Jerry Franklin Poe
beinspired@jerrypoe.com
Founder of ItsYourPersonality.com

Mark wrote the "Grow Your Local Business" column for Dan Kennedy's No BS Marketing Letter

Mark spoke at Perry Marshall's Rainmaker Event in Chicago

Mark worked for the late, great Walter
Payton in Chicago in the 90s

TABLE OF CONTENTS

FOREWORD

Revenue keeps a business running, but profit changes lives. Nobody wants to earn money only to stay afloat. We all desire stability, opportunities, and a legacy for our families. It starts with one key idea: **Know your worth.**

Who are you? Why should people listen to you? What problem do you solve?

If you are not deliberate in answering these questions, your audience will move on to someone else who is. The marketplace is not looking for more content; it's looking for meaningful content. Content that educates, solves problems, and positions you as the authority. Creating content just to stay visible is a waste of time. Creating content with purpose is how you become known.

When you align your message with your value, and your value with your audience's needs, you create **cashflow.** Mark Imperial's *Cashflow Content* challenges you to think differently, act intentionally, and position yourself with clarity. Having experienced Mark's perspective firsthand, I can say with confidence that his approach is both practical and powerful. His book is a must-read for anyone serious about turning knowledge into influence, and influence into real, measurable results.

If you're ready to elevate your voice, own your value, and become known for what you know, you're in good hands.

Carl E. Brown, Jr.
State/Executive Director
District of Columbia Small Business Development Center
carl.brown@howard.edu | www.dcsbdc.org
Host, "The Small Business Report" – SIRIUS XM Channel 141
As seen on History Channel's "The Food That Built America," The Wall Street Journal, and MSNBC

INTRODUCTION

WHY CASHFLOW CONTENT EXISTS

*The Creator Economy Was Never
Built for Business Owners*

....

"Doubt is not a pleasant condition, but certainty is absurd."

—VOLTAIRE

....

Something about how content is discussed today doesn't sit right. The advice is loud and constant. *"Post every day!" "Feed the algorithm!" "Use keywords in your headlines for SEO!" "Grow your audience, then monetize!"* Sound familiar? The expectations feel strangely disconnected from how real businesses actually operate.

If you've ever felt like the entire content conversation is slightly off, but couldn't quite explain why, this book is for you. Because if content truly worked the way it's sold, more smart, capable business owners wouldn't feel this uneasy about it.

WHY MOST CONTENT ADVICE
FAILS REAL BUSINESS OWNERS

It is rarely acknowledged that most content advice wasn't created for business owners in the first place. Much of it is parroted from the new generation and not rooted in the fundamentals of true branding and marketing communications. Positioning and differentiation are often overlooked, resulting in generic content that dilutes a brand's unique identity. This advice was built for creators, influencers, and media-first careers. People whose "intended" business *is* content. Business owners were invited into that world without the fine print, risking valuable hours and potentially squeezing profitability in exchange for the illusion of expanded reach.

So when posting daily feels forced…
When chasing trends feels distracting…
When the return on effort never quite matches the promise…
It's easy to assume the problem is *you.*
That you're inconsistent. That you're not "doing it right."
That you're resistant, maybe "too old for this nonsense!"
That you just haven't "committed" enough yet.

But the issue isn't effort. The issue is **misapplied models**. Most business owners are operating with a gap they can't quite see. They've got real skills. They've earned their wisdom the hard way. They know they're damn good at what they do. Their clients get incredible results and rave about them… when they find them. But they are not *known* for it.

I call this the **Known-For Gap.**

It's the distance between your actual expertise and what the market recognizes you for. And until that gap is closed, your content feels like effort without return. You were handed a framework designed for attention-based careers and told to make it work for a revenue-based business. That mismatch creates friction. The goal of this book is to remove that friction and replace it with clarity. I will show you how to close that gap without becoming a full-time creator.

THE CREATOR-ECONOMY DREAM VS. BUSINESS REALITY

The creator economy runs on a simple narrative:

Build attention first. Monetize later. (Wait, what?)
Let platforms do the heavy lifting. "The algorithm!" (Ugh!)
Volume wins. (Double ugh!)

This model is designed for creators who are playing that game intentionally. Even then, it works for a minuscule few, leaving others with only a bounty of wasted time.

I'm not here to bash creators because they aren't the problem. The problem is the creator-economy myth being applied to business owners. Businesses operate under a different reality:

Revenue comes first.
Communication supports sales.
Platforms are media distribution, not strategy.
Being intentional beats volume.

A business doesn't need to be famous. It needs to be trusted, recognized, and remembered at the right moment. When this happens, you're no longer explaining what you do. People already associate you with it. They trust your judgment. They think of you at the right moment.

I call this the **Known-For Effect.**

It's what happens when your expertise is clearly expressed, consistently seen, and easily remembered. Trust builds faster. Demand shows up sooner. And the right opportunities start to find you.

CASHFLOW IS RESPONSIBILITY

Somewhere along the way, talking about cashflow became uncomfortable, as if focusing on revenue meant you were less authentic, less principled, and less mission-driven; that you were someone trying to sell something. Well, duh!

That's nonsense.

Cashflow isn't greed if it's ethical. And *ethical* greed *is* good. Ask Michael Douglas. I have an expression: *"If you enrich people's lives 10 times to 100 times what you ask in return, the world would be a better place."* Would you agree?

Cashflow is payroll. That payroll feeds families, who then go out into the world and, hopefully, do good and spread their wealth to other businesses in the community and around the world.

Money isn't inherently good or bad. It just moves around. Some over here. Some over there. Some ducks in my pond. Some ducks in other ponds. I like to think, *"I know I'll do good with those ducks, so it's better there are more in my pond."* If you do good for the world, I want you to get lots of ducks, too.

If your business gives the value I'm talking about, taking money from someone won't diminish their fortune or status. It should give them more fortune and raise their status.

Cashflow gives you peace of mind. It offers stability, optionality, and the ability to say no to the wrong work and yes to the right opportunities.

For business owners, cashflow is a responsibility. And content that doesn't contribute to cashflow is negligent. That doesn't mean every post needs to sell. It just means that communication should serve a purpose, which brings us to the real problem with how content is framed today.

CONTENT IS AN ASSET, NOT A PERFORMANCE

Most people are taught to experience content as a performance. You show up. You post. You hope it lands. And then, almost as quickly, it disappears into the feed, replaced by whatever comes next.

Performances are fleeting by design. They exist in the moment and fade the second attention moves on. Assets behave differently. They build upon themselves, much like interest that accrues on a savings account while you sleep. This compounding effect means that assets retain their value, carry it forward, and continue to work long after the initial effort is over.

The most effective content should grab the attention of those for which it was intended; it should enter the conversation already going on in their minds; it should bond you with them because they can see your values match theirs; it should anchor you in their mind for a unique position that they value so you will always be top of mind for that thing you do, or for that solution they desperately need.

The reason this content is so effective is that it "captures" your thinking, documenting your judgment and recording your standards. It provides clear answers to real questions that buyers are already asking.

When content is treated as something to be built rather than performed, it stops feeling exhausting. You're no longer feeding an algorithm or chasing relevance. You're constructing something that works for you repeatedly, without requiring you to show up every time.

This is where most conversations about content miss the mark. They obsess over output: how often to post, what format to use, how to stay visible, while ignoring the infrastructure underneath.

Gary Halbert famously said, "Motion beats meditation." He was right. But only if that motion is efficient. And efficiency only comes when content is designed as an asset from the start, not treated like a performance you have to repeat forever.

THE BOUNDARIES OF THIS BOOK

Before we go any further, it's worth defining what you're holding.

This book is a doctrine. It lays out a way of thinking that governs how content is created, used, and sustained over time. It's a system, not a schedule. A framework for judgment, not a calendar filled with prompts.

You won't find generic posting plans or surface-level advice here. This book is written for people who sell real things to real clients, and who want their communication to support that reality rather than distract from it.

Its focus isn't the creator economy or social-media theatrics. It isn't concerned with chasing reach, riding trends, or manufacturing virality. Those approaches come and go. Foundational assets endure. We'll focus on clarity, alignment, and a calm, sustainable way to stay present in your market.

THE MESSENGER MATTERS
MORE IN AN AGE OF AI

We also need to address the giant purple gorilla in the room. In the age of AI, some wonder if the overwhelming flood of content now being generated will make it irrelevant, just more digital junk mail. The opposite is true. When information becomes abundant and instantly produced, the message becomes a commodity, but the messenger becomes <u>invaluable</u>. AI can produce words. It cannot replace judgment, lived experience, standards, sequencing, or perspective.

As tools get smarter, people will search harder for recognizable voices they trust. The sherpas, the guides. The AI era is not a threat to you. It is a gift if you are sharp enough to see it and disciplined enough to memorialize how you think. If you have considered this the age of the "Creator," then I declare that we are now moving into the age of the Navigator. **"The Navigator Economy."**

CONTENT IS INFRASTRUCTURE, NOT JUST POSTING

We need to expand what the word "content" actually means. Content is not just YouTube videos or social media posts. Content is any deliberate expression of your thinking designed to attract, educate, or move someone toward a decision. It includes articles, emails, interviews, presentations, podcasts, and yes, books. A book, in particular, is the apex asset because it distills your perspective into a permanent doorway into your world. Everything else can orbit around it. When done properly, content isn't noise. It's infrastructure.

HOW THIS BOOK IS DESIGNED TO WORK

This book unfolds in three parts...intentionally.

❖ **Part One** removes the broken models that made content feel confusing, frustrating, and like a distraction from the real work of growing your business. The ones that make you think: *This is too much work. I don't want to learn another thing. Why am I even doing this?*

❖ **Part Two** helps you clarify what already works, only better: your thinking, your standards, your judgment. The process of capturing what makes you different, giving it a name, and turning it into a signature way of doing things others can recognize and choose is what I call *"Memorialize Your Magic."* This concept was born from the realization that the unique elements of your business should be celebrated and preserved. By framing, naming and claiming this process, it becomes a defining feature of how you deliver value, ensuring that your distinctive qualities are consistently communicated.

❖ **Part Three** shows how to take the magic you've defined and turn it into a simple, repeatable system that consistently reaches the right people and drives customers.

Along the way, we'll answer questions most business owners are already asking:

- *Do I really have to post so much for this to work?*
- *Why does content feel like a second job instead of part of my business?*
- *Is there a way to stay visible without turning into a content creator?*
- *Is any of this actually going to bring in customers?*

THE CORE DOCTRINE OF CASHFLOW CONTENT

At its core, this book is built on a simple belief:

If content doesn't contribute to cashflow, it's a distraction.

Cashflow Content won't lecture you on "just showing up" or pushing louder messages the way so many talking heads do. To be fair, as filmmaker Woody Allen once said, *"Eighty percent of success is showing up."* That's true. But how you arrive determines whether someone leans in or swipes past you and unsubscribes.

When you show up, are you a helpful friend or an annoying pest?

This book centers on relevant communication; being genuinely useful at the moment someone actually needs you. It's attention paired with action. Visibility with purpose. Consistency guided by intention.

Content isn't the business. It exists to support the business you already run. Its job is to keep you present and relevant, build trust, and help the right people recognize you when the timing is right. If you know communication matters but refuse to let it become a distraction, a performance, or a second career, keep reading.

To understand why the current content story became the default, and why it never really fit...

We need to start at the beginning...

—Mark Imperial

PART ONE

THE CONTENT MYTH

WHY THE ADVICE BUSINESS OWNERS FOLLOW KEEPS THEM INVISIBLE

. . . .

"Context omitted is a seed from
which misunderstandings sprout."
—UNKNOWN AUTHOR

THE CREATOR ECONOMY LIE

Why Business Owners Have Been Given the Wrong Content Playbook

....

"There is nothing so useless as doing efficiently that which should not be done at all."

—PETER DRUCKER

....

Imagine waking up each morning with a sense of dread, feeling the weight of time slipping away, and the spark of your business's spirit dimming. Over the last few years, I've observed a dangerous trend that threatens the core of what makes both individuals and businesses thrive. This trend is robbing them of their two most precious assets: their time and their spirit. Let me tell you what I've seen.

I sponsor general and niche business conferences to generate clients for my book publishing business, where I help business leaders turn what they know into what they want to be known for. I've had a booth and occasionally spoken at conferences for DJs, attorneys, business brokers, and other professional service providers. Then I began adding creator conferences aimed at folks like podcasters and YouTubers, knowing that a book would be the fastest and smartest way for them to establish their brand, whether they were new or not. People were already expecting books from established podcasters and YouTubers, and newbies could definitely leapfrog to the top by having a book. Thousands of people attended these conferences, and here's what triggered my alarm after speaking to these audiences and talking to many at our booth...

Many people start "creating," whether podcasting or YouTubing, or whatever, because they believe they are growing a huge audience to *maybe eventually* get "sponsorship money." Or get paid for "views" somehow.

Many, if not most, of the "creators" I met didn't even have a real business. They thought the show that they were starting was going to BE the business. Although a signature book would undoubtedly be the vehicle that could anchor their topic in the mind of their audience and grow whatever they were doing faster and more efficiently than anything else, most of them barely had a grasp on why they were even doing this podcast thing in the first place. They were in the "stick a toe in the water" phase, so very few had the level of commitment to even prioritize writing a book. Most of them had one foot in their creator role and another foot on a banana peel. This lack of clarity and commitment highlights a critical insight: to succeed truly, creators need to establish a solid foundation and a clear purpose for their endeavors, much like how a signature book grounds their topic and amplifies their influence. Without this foundation, they risk their efforts having no meaningful impact.

The feeling I got was that, because they were sold on the "podcasting is free" dream, most of them were in the "let's see how this goes first, otherwise I can just quit, no big deal mode." That is a weak prospect for a book publishing offer. This is akin to making offers to freebie seekers. Wrong room.

What's worse is that the business owners attending the conference were under the illusion that they were receiving valuable content marketing training, unaware that they had become ensnared by the "Creator-Only Guru" trap. This misguided direction, championed by people who favor algorithms over actual business strategies, meant that they didn't even realize they were in the wrong place. The information being peddled was geared towards turning content into a business, not enhancing a business owner's existing visibility and promoting what they're already selling. This unintentional deception is what I found most alarming.

Don't get me wrong, it isn't the creator conferences or the creators themselves who are at fault. They evolved a framework that may work for them. That framework just has not come with any translation for the business owner. A lot of what creators do can seem like "extra" to the business owner.

Further clues were hidden in plain sight…

At these creator conferences, I would attend the opening-night party to get a look at the inhabitants. Each year, the host would typically ask into the microphone, *"Raise your hand if this is your first [insert name of whatever conference]!"* Since you learn more from looking around the room than from looking at the host, I would diligently watch how many hands would go up.

Maybe I shouldn't have been shocked, but it was usually over 90% of the room. Then I would think, *"Holy crap, they must be amazing marketers if they can get all these new people."* But then my amazement turned to shock and suspicion, *"Holy crap, what happened to all the people from last year?"*

I know it doesn't work this way in the real world, but theoretically, if you had a thousand people last year who were all successful, and you have a thousand new people this year, then you should have 2,000 people, LOL.

So what happened? As far as I can surmise from my experience, the data, and my amateur sleuthing, 90% are the people who stuck their toe in the water last year, then quit and took up crochet.

The creator economy content marketing advice was the only advice out there, and it started to sound the same.

"You need to be posting more."
"You need to build an audience."
"You need to show up every day."
"You need to become a creator."

And at first, it didn't sound unreasonable. After all, visibility *does* matter. Staying present *does* matter. Businesses that disappear from the conversation *do* get forgotten.

So you tried. You posted when you could. You followed the advice. You experimented with formats, platforms, and frequencies. But you also posted what you were having for lunch and (hopefully not) bathroom selfies.

And then something strange happened. The effort increased, but the business didn't. The work felt real. The time investment felt heavy. The return felt vague or non-existent. The juice wasn't worth the squeeze. You couldn't pay the mortgage with likes, nor deposit them in the bank. Views may have spiked, but who are the viewers? Comments felt nice and made you feel like you were doing something, but rarely turned into conversations that mattered.

And quietly, without announcing itself, a thought crept in: *"This isn't working the way it's supposed to."*

That thought was usually followed by reflection, and maybe guilt. *"Am I doing this right? Am I being consistent enough? Maybe I need to post more. Maybe I just haven't cracked the algorithm yet."* Gotta love that one.

So you either pushed harder or pulled away entirely. Most business owners don't quit content because they're lazy. They quit because something felt off. More importantly, the effort didn't ring the cash register.

For many, it seemed wrong to dismiss it entirely as "content doesn't work!"

Here's what no one said clearly at the time: You weren't failing at content. You were succeeding at a model that was never designed for you. And the only action it was designed for was content consumption, not buying behavior. The advice you were following came from a different world where attention *is* the product, and monetization happens later, if at all.

That world is called the Creator Economy.

And while it works *sometimes* for people who choose it intentionally, it quietly breaks business owners who are pulled into it by default.

Because when your livelihood depends on real clients, real trust, and real timing, "just create more" isn't a strategy. It's a distraction dressed up as discipline. The lie was that becoming a creator was the only way to make content work.

HOW "BE A CREATOR" BECAME THE DEFAULT ADVICE

The creator economy didn't begin as a lie. It began as a solution. A legit solution. To understand how we came to this, we have to examine the evolution. What I'm about to share will show you that I'm not some new internet cowboy, but an OG that understands <u>all media</u> and where it fits.

Take it from me, an OG that sent his first marketing messages using stamps on envelopes and even sent FAX sales letters! Remember those? That makes me sound like a caveman etching sales letters on stone tablets using rocks.

My point? Back in those days, the only way that you could get attention for your business was to pay a lot of money for very few things that were available to you: Print advertising in newspapers or magazines, direct mail, TV or radio ads, or billboards on the side of the road.

Everything changed with the advent of the internet. Remember the promise of the internet? *"This is going to level the playing field!"* It started with websites! *"Now everybody can have a beautiful storefront on the information superhighway! This is no longer reserved for just people with big budgets that can afford a brick-and-mortar building and a beautiful sign!"*

OMG, I remember my first website for my DJ business. Wow, it was horrific. I was like a kid with the family-size carton of crayons, and nobody told me I shouldn't use every color. Don't get me started on the nifty code I learned so everyone's cursor would leave little animated trails on my website. LOL. Hey, it was the 90's!

But it still wasn't "creator central" because blogs weren't yet widespread, and video wasn't a thing yet.

The next two revolutions are really what brought us here—social media and online video. Social media came along in the late 90s with a platform most won't know or remember called SixDegrees, which was way ahead of its time when only 18% of households had the internet, let alone knew what to do with it. Shortly afterwards, more familiar names like Friendster in 2002, MySpace and LinkedIn in 2003, and, of course, Facebook in 2004, exploded in popularity as users grew comfortable with the internet (thank you, AOL).

The biggest leap came from online video! The dancing baby got everyone talking. I bought my first online video course from Jim Edwards and Mike Stewart around 2005 or 2006, and that changed the direction of my life! I think even in the course, Jim and Mike said, *"There's this new thing, YouTube, that could be useful."* LOL. Even before YouTube, I put my first video on my website using some weird code and video players that I learned from the course. I remember the reaction from my clients and prospects was, *"Wow, how did you do that?"* I was then the cool kid, and my DJ business blew up. I was the first in my area to put party photos from each of the Bar Mitzvahs we did on our website. People loved it, and that's when I discovered that people flocked to my site to see their party pics, and BOOM! Built-in word-of-mouth. That was circa 1998. I guess I was being a creator before creator was a thing. I always used the expression "I'm a creator" because I created and launched ideas into businesses. Now, the word has a different connotation. I digress.

Then, around 2006, YouTube made it so much easier to put a video online and share it without needing all the goofy codes and video players. My first use of YouTube was to post testimonials from my customers and clients, and that really brought them to life vs. the old words on paper. Like most things, it started out tactical until people figured out how to be strategic.

What the hell was my point, and what was I trying to say?

Oh yeah. The internet began to evolve into a usable, essentially free medium you could use to grow your business! Did it really level the playing field? Depends on how you look at it. Yes, now the average business owner can DIY marketing messages on the internet that will sit right next to Fortune 500 commercials that cost $500,000 to produce. But at the same time, it expanded the playing field, and every Tom, Dick, and Harry (and my neighbor's 10-year-old) is putting stuff out that brings up a new challenge—drowning in a sea of content.

Here's where it started to get weird…

The platforms knew that, to succeed, they needed to attract and retain users.

Platforms needed content.

Content needed creators.

Creators needed incentive.

If you were making stuff for the platforms, you were a "creator." Maybe even an "influencer." So *attention* was framed as opportunity. The platforms rewarded creators for keeping users' attention long enough to insert their paid ads, because that was a major part of their monetization. This alone shifted people's perceptions of the platforms' use.

"Oh, I can get paid $5 if 1,000 people watch my video? That's $5,000 for a million views! Wow, I'll be rich!" Boom, a new game was created.

But it distracted business owners from the original objective—*"Let's sell some of our shit!"*

With that in mind, can you see why the people now teaching "Here's how to make content" can be seen as teaching it for a reason other than what a business owner needs it for?

They're teaching:

→ Post consistently.
→ Grow an audience.
→ Monetize later.

For people whose product *is* content, this made sense. Again, doesn't make them wrong or bad, just not the right plan for a business owner who can monetize now by selling their services or products, not waiting for ad revenue pennies to add up. Views were inventory. Followers were leverage. Sponsorships and ads were the business model.

But then something subtle happened. That advice escaped its original context. It was repeated, simplified, and amplified until "be a creator" became shorthand for "this is how visibility works now." Business owners heard it and thought, *I guess this is just how things are.*

No one stopped to say:
"This model assumes attention *is* the product."

No one added the footnote:
"This only works if you can wait to build an audience and revenue isn't dependent on anybody buying your shit!"

And so business owners entered a game whose rules were never written for them.

WHY GETTING PAID FOR VIEWS WAS NEVER A BUSINESS PLAN

Maybe it was easier for me to see because I'm old school. If it didn't make dollars, it didn't make sense. This is where the business owners who were astute in direct response marketing and branding really could leverage these platforms. In direct response marketing, we are always looking for the quickest path to the sale.

The formula was straightforward before the internet. I could place an ad in a magazine or direct mail a postcard or letter offering a free report, which was basically a sales letter in disguise. The people would respond, and I would mail them a package that would make them want to purchase a solution to the problem I described. That package could include an audio CD or a DVD (back in the day, it was a cassette tape or VHS!), and it would most certainly include a long-form multi-page sales letter along with an order form.

You see, we had two elements going there: attention, which led to interest. When I mailed them the sales letter package, it was designed to create desire, and that desire led to the action of purchasing what was offered in the letter. Simple.

How does that translate to the modern-day content warrior?

Attention doesn't equal readiness. And it doesn't automatically lead to an audience! Views don't equal demand. Reach doesn't equal trust. An algorithm can show your message to thousands of people who will never care, want, or need what you sell. And even when they *do* need it someday, attention alone doesn't preserve timing.

Creators survive this reality because they play a volume game. *(Or they can tolerate waiting and feeling like they're doing something. After all, many people mistake activity for accomplishment).*

Business owners can't afford to and shouldn't have to.

A business or professional service doesn't need millions of views. It needs the *right* people to recognize it at the *right* moment. That's not an attention problem; it's a communication problem. The creator economy optimizes for novelty. Businesses should optimize for recognition, relevance, trust, and action (response). Which essentially describes the term I coined, "ActionBranding."

The creator economy rewards volume. Businesses benefit from a short, clear path to a sale. Those are not the same incentives, and pretending they are creates frustration in place of growth.

WHEN OUTPUT DOESN'T PRODUCE OUTCOMES, QUITTING IS RATIONAL

Back in the day, a controversial expression in advertising was that you needed repetition and loads of exposure to make a sale. That wasn't much different than the creator economy mantra of "volume" today. Thinking that the more you post, the more sales and revenue you will have.

When business owners burn out on content, it's usually framed as a motivation issue. They "couldn't stay consistent." They "lost momentum." They "fell off." That framing misses the point. Burnout is more about misalignment than effort. It's about "This effort didn't bring any measurable result, so why should I continue to do this?"

When the work required doesn't match the return promised, discipline turns into resentment. Posting feels like feeding a machine instead of building an asset. Showing up feels like performance instead of communication. So people quit. Resistance, in this case, isn't laziness. It's smartly recognizing you need to pivot.

CREATORS VS. BUSINESS OWNER CREATORS

To move forward, we need a clean distinction.

Creators optimize for reach, for attention; for the latest gimmick. Business owners optimize for relevance. Creators chase platforms and the almighty algorithm. Business owners build assets.

Creators ask, *"How do I get more eyeballs?"* Business owners ask, *"How do the right people recognize me when it matters (when people most need my solution and are ready to buy)?"*

Same tools. Different jobs. This book isn't anti-creator. It's anti-confusion. Because when business owners are told to act like creators, they end up doing more work for less clarity and calling it progress.

The new breed of business owner who leverages content and content platforms is known as a **Business Owner Creator.** This is a business-first, performance-second creator. Instead of relying on clickbait and trying to game the algorithm, business owner creators are strategic and deliberate about the content they create. Every piece of content has a job. The good news is, any business that has been around a while likely already has many of the pieces of this puzzle, and they don't even know it.

Working with my mentor, Dan Kennedy, he taught me that the term "new media" is just a fancy way to say "another channel of communication." People who started businesses on the internet called themselves internet marketers, which is funny because, before the internet, I owned a DJ company that used the Yellow Pages as one of our media channels to attract leads. Yet, I didn't call myself a Yellow Pages marketer.

The internet is nothing more than another media channel or a collection of media channels, depending on how you want to look at it. However, if cable television once felt overwhelming with its 10,000 channels compared to the only 4 major broadcast networks, the internet takes that fragmentation to an exponential level. Today, instead of a handful of networks or even hundreds of cable stations, we seemingly face millions of micro-channels — each social platform, podcast, YouTube creator, newsletter, or niche community represents its own media outlet. This explosion of options means audiences are no longer concentrated in predictable places; they scatter across interest-based tribes and individual influencers.

For marketers and communicators, that means two things: First, reaching a broad audience requires stitching together dozens of smaller, highly targeted efforts rather than relying on a few mass outlets. Second, success depends on understanding where your specific audience actually spends its time and how it prefers to consume information. The challenge isn't just producing content — it's navigating this fragmented landscape with precision and authenticity, finding signal amid near-infinite noise.

When there were only four major broadcast networks, the average business owner could not afford the fee to advertise on any of them. Now, the good news is that many micro channels are affordable for the small business owner, and your game plan can be to stitch together a few, or what I call, "puddle jump," and bootstrap your rollout over time, smartly, with cashflow.

The Business Owner Creator recognizes these fundamentals. They aren't reinventing the wheel; they're merely repurposing what we already have, adjusting it for different platforms.

FOLLOWING THE RULES AND STILL ENDING UP FLAT ON YOUR BACK

The real damage of the creator economy is eroded confidence (not to mention the time you waste). Eroded trust in the teachers of this "new media" gives you that feeling Charlie Brown has when he runs up to the football every time to have Lucy pull it away so he falls on his ass.

When business owners repeatedly show up, follow the rules, and don't see meaningful results, they start questioning their judgment. They second-guess what they know. Worse, they quit. They pull the plug on any attempt to stay relevant. They don't even go back to old school advertising or marketing because now they're convinced "that doesn't work anymore." Being paralyzed in inaction is the path to a slow death.

ARE YOU READY TO FINALLY GET THIS RIGHT?

If this chapter feels relieving, that's intentional. Its job wasn't to give you a new strategy. It was to take away a bad one. To name the lie clearly. To remove guilt quietly. To validate the instinct that said, *"Doing this content creator thing isn't for me, it's weird."*

Because before content can work, the model has to fit the business. And before content assets that drive sales can compound, clarity has to come first.

I can likely assume that many business owners reading this book just realized they were following the creator economy formula and making the wrong content for the wrong reasons. I know it's not your fault. It's what you've been sold. You're welcome.

In the next chapter, we'll look at what actually breaks when attention is prioritized without action and why most businesses stall right there.

Only then can we talk about what content is *supposed* to do.

KEY TAKEAWAYS

- The creator economy wasn't built for business owners who need clients, trust, and timing *now,* not *someday.*

- Attention, views, and consistency don't, on their own, equal readiness, demand, or sales.

- Most content burnout comes from playing a game whose rules were never designed for how real businesses make money.

- Business owners need content that supports what they already sell.

- The problem was never with content itself; it was following a model that optimized consumption instead of action.

- We are moving away from being a creator to becoming a **Business Owner Creator.**

CHAPTER

WHY CONTENT FAILS

Visibility Without Conversion Doesn't Pay

···

"It would be too easy to say that I feel invisible.
Instead, I feel painfully visible, and entirely ignored."
—DAVID LEVITHAN, AUTHOR

···

This chapter turns empty visibility into revenue-moving clarity. With the confusion of the creator economy cleared up in Chapter One, we can now narrow the focus.

By this point, you may be thinking...
If attention isn't the goal, what is?
And why does so much content still feel busy but ineffective?

Simple. The goal should be outcomes (clarity, resonance, conversions, trust), not raw attention. Most businesses would say a positive outcome means selling more. But outcomes operate in layers. At one layer, growth comes from acquiring more prospects at the top of the funnel. At a deeper level, it comes from selling more to your raving fans (people who have already bought from you). Growth compounds when those raving fans begin telling others about you, naturally feeding the top of your funnel. And beyond that, it's about nurturing new prospects until the timing is right for them to buy. We'll explore these layers in more detail in Part Three of this book. Visibility alone isn't the problem. It's visibility without direction. Phones don't ring. Calendars don't fill. Conversations don't advance. And yet, the metrics say they're "doing well." That contradiction is where frustration lives.

THE SEDUCTION OF VANITY METRICS

"When you are up to your neck in alligators, it is difficult to remind yourself that your initial objective was to drain the swamp."
—Anonymous

The numbers that some would tell you indicate that you're doing well, even if they're not linked to any sales, are called "vanity metrics." Consider Brand X: They had 1 million views on their promotional video, yet it resulted in zero sales. This illustrates how vanity metrics can create a false sense of success. They are seductive because they *feel* like progress in the form of likes, views, followers, and shares.

Which is exactly the problem.

Those things alone are just indicators. They don't tell you much until you can accurately tell me how many of those converted into an actual sale. Vanity metrics give emotional feedback without economic consequence. They tell you *something* happened, but not whether it mattered.

A post can perform beautifully and still do nothing for your business. In fact, there are tons of "successful" posts that don't make a single sale or advance any business objectives because algorithms reward novelty, while businesses rely on familiarity.

The more you optimize for what performs, the more you drift from what converts. If you start chasing more likes and views, you inadvertently trade off conversions for clickbait. And without realizing it, you begin confusing movement with momentum.

WHY "BUILD AN AUDIENCE FIRST" STALLS REAL BUSINESSES

One of the most common pieces of advice business owners hear is this:

"Just focus on building an audience. The rest will come later."

You already have a real business with real products and services to offer, so why do you need to delay selling something?

That advice sounds like it's meant for creators. *"Let's build an audience of people who love pug puppies, and we'll figure out what to sell them later, maybe t-shirts."* In practice, that's how business owners end up with a feeling like **"Pugs Got the Likes. Bills Still Due."** Plenty of attention, but nothing actually moves.

Imagine someone with a huge problem stumbles onto one of your pieces of content that provides exactly the fix they need. At that moment, they're not interested in being part of an audience; they want a solution to their problem. This is where effective content can turn that need into an opportunity for connection and conversion.

If your content followed the latest trend, you may grow your numbers because your version of the trend entertains people, but you wouldn't have shown up for them when they were looking for a solution to their problem. This is the very distraction I am trying to help you avoid.

Audiences don't buy; *people* do. And people buy when timing, trust, and relevance converge. Most audiences are curious, not committed. When businesses prioritize audience growth over buyer readiness, they end up serving the wrong moment in the decision cycle. They entertain when people need clarity. They inspire when people need certainty. And when nothing moves, the answer is always the same:

"You just need more people."

That belief keeps businesses busy and stuck.

Consider this: Are your followers cheering for your brand, or are they merely checking it out? This question can prompt an important self-assessment. Are you reaching the right people at the right time, or are you stuck with an audience that isn't ready to engage or purchase?

ALGORITHM CHASING VS. BUYER READINESS

First, I won't assume too much. Some of you may be thinking, "What the heck do they mean when they say 'algorithm' anyway???"

The platform's algorithm's job is to keep people on their platform, not to help you build a business (kind of a split loyalty, huh?) First, redirect your thinking from platform triggers to buyer troubles. Instead of wondering, *"What will trigger the algorithm to make my video go viral?"* ask *"What troubles my perfect prospect the most?"*

The algorithms reward:

→ Novelty
→ Frequency
→ Engagement velocity

They don't reward:

→ Judgment
→ Timing
→ Trust

Buyer readiness is quiet. It doesn't spike or announce itself. It reveals itself over time through recognition. Your tribe is silently nodding their heads and saying, *"This person gets me!"* When someone sees your thinking repeatedly, when your perspective matches their problem precisely, and when your standards feel familiar before the conversation even begins, that triggers readiness. And no algorithm can manufacture it. The tragedy is that the more businesses chase reach, the less grounded they feel in their own message.

They do weird stuff and make novelty videos. They chase the latest trend and make their own version of the ALS ice bucket challenge, or they make plain vanilla videos just to be "frequent." In trying to appeal to everyone, they become indistinguishable to the people who matter most.

THE MOST EXPENSIVE "FREE" MISTAKE IN MARKETING

Free content is costing you more than you think. The advice today is dangerous: *"Just post more,"* *"It's free, if it doesn't work, it hardly costs you,"* or *"Testing that used to cost a lot is now FREE, so take advantage!"* The very access to a "level playing field" is quietly destroying those who naively think they're taking advantage of it. Sure, sending a message today may only cost you the time to produce it and any delivery costs, whether email, social, text, or whatever. But let's talk about the real cost. First, some history…

There was a time when putting a message into the world meant something. Ads cost money. Mail costs money. Media costs money. So people were careful. They studied what worked. They modeled proven winners because it cost so much to find the winners (in ad costs that didn't work), and if an ad kept running, you knew one thing: It worked.

Today? You can post instantly. Test endlessly. Delete and move on. No "perceived" cost. No commitment. And because the cost disappeared, so did the discipline. Now we live in a world of careless content. People say things less intentionally. They post ideas they haven't thought through, and jump from message to message as if none of it matters. But it does.

It may only become obvious once I point it out (I always say some of life's biggest clues are hidden in plain sight). Let's talk about the invisible cost of that slop: **Loss of attention. Damage to reputation. Essentially, staying or returning to INVISIBLE.** When your ideas feel disposable, your authority becomes forgettable. And you train the market to ignore you.

So how do you avoid this trap? Try this:

What if every post cost you $1,000? You'd slow down. You'd think. You'd make it count. Because you are paying in time, attention, reputation, and real money. Every piece of content either builds your authority or chips away at it. So stop treating content like it's free. If you do just one thing, treat every piece of content as if it cost you *everything*. You'll already be lightyears ahead of your competition. Because cheap content creates expensive consequences. Treat your content like it doesn't matter, and the market will follow your lead.

YOU ARE NOW A BUSINESS OWNER CREATOR

If you've ever felt awkward trying to make content, or it just makes you cringe at the thought of making content, you're not alone. It's not natural, and if you came from the OG world, the only thing you thought you needed to do was run some advertising, which was probably print and a sales letter.

But don't worry, that instinct may just be serving you! You may be looking at it from the wrong angle. Perhaps you saw a Mr. Beast or

Jake Paul video and thought, *"How the heck are these people successful? All they're doing is making videos about weird stuff!"*

You wouldn't be wrong, but remember that they are doing it for a different reason than you. They're doing it backwards. They're trying to create a personal brand around themselves, and they figure they'll find something to sell you later. But for a business owner, that type of observation is distracting! Stop! Cancel! Don't look at those types of folks as models.

Business owner creators are going to focus on making only the type of content they would have made in print, in an advertisement, on their website copy, or something else that would have served their people. As a business owner creator, you have an advantage. You already have a product or service to sell, so you already know who you should be talking to. Just like a GPS, now you can reverse-engineer all the stuff you need to make it to that destination.

Business owners resist content when it feels performative and pulls them away from real work. Professionals resist becoming entertainers. Experts resist nonsense. You're not crazy! Your alarm bells are going off. When the content's frame is wrong, no amount of tactics will fix that feeling.

THE HIDDEN COST OF ATTENTION WITHOUT ACTION

The most damaging part of attention-first content is that it not only wastes time but also drains your spirit as a business owner. When you show up consistently, and nothing meaningful happens, you start questioning what you're doing. You lose faith in your instincts.

You forget what makes you distinctive. You hesitate to make clear statements. You soften your offers to avoid alienating the audience. Over time, content stops reflecting how you actually think. It becomes generic, or, worse, copycat.

Not to mention, you will be gathering a questionable herd that you've trained to be unresponsive! Who are these people anyway? Did they tune you out? How valuable are the non-responsive?

That's what happens when communication is separated from purpose.

WHAT CONTENT WAS NEVER MEANT TO DO

Content was never meant to entertain strangers indefinitely. It wasn't meant to convince anyone or manufacture demand. And it definitely wasn't meant to replace meaningful conversations. It should do just the opposite: trigger them! Content exists to support decisions. It's supposed to clarify, educate, solidify trust over time, and establish brand footprints.

When content is disconnected from action, it becomes noise. Noise, no matter how loud, eventually gets tuned out.

THE REAL QUESTION TO ASK

If attention alone doesn't move a business...
If audiences don't guarantee readiness...
If performance doesn't build trust...

Then the real question isn't: *"How do I get more visibility?"*

It's: *"What should my content actually be doing, day after day, to support my business?"*

That's the question most content advice never answers. And it's the question we'll answer next. Because once you see what content is *supposed* to do, everything else changes.

KEY TAKEAWAYS

- Visibility matters only when it drives movement toward real business outcomes.

- Metrics are useful when they connect to judgment, trust, and decision-making, not just activity.

- People engage and buy when your perspective meets their problem at the right moment.

- Discomfort with performative content commonly indicates professionalism and clarity about who you serve.

- Content works best when it supports decisions, strengthens trust, and advances real conversations.

THE "KNOWN-FOR GAP"

*The Distance Between What You Know
and What You're "Known-For"*

....

*"We don't see things as they are,
we see them as we are."*

—ANAIS NIN

....

If you have just begun exploring the idea of content creation and distribution for your business, then the good news is that this book will save you a lot of time in trial and error. By the time most business owners reach this point, they've already tried enough content advice and feel either confused or frustrated. They've posted consistently. They've experimented with platforms. They've followed the formulas, the trends, and the "best practices," including nonsense advice like *"Use SEO keywords in your headlines and titles of your videos!"* And nothing seems to be doing anything as a result of their efforts.

The problem is that business owners have learned to create the wrong content for the wrong reasons. You shouldn't be worried about how to post or where to post until you consider *what job content is actually supposed to do* inside a real business. Also, most creator-type training isn't steeped in the fundamentals of direct response marketing, which is what you actually need to ring the cash register.

Until those two things are addressed, everything else stays stuck in the mud.

THE "KNOWN-FOR" GAP

Like many professionals, you might think you have a marketing problem or a visibility problem. You've been told to be more consistent with your content (there's that vague term again!) You think you need "better" content. Or to use more platforms. You may assume the fame (and success) goes to those who publish the most.

That's NOT the problem! The problem is much simpler.

You are likely suffering from what I call the **Known-For Gap**, which is the distance between what you know and what the market knows you for. You already have wisdom. You know things. You've solved problems, developed opinions, and methods for doing the things you do. You've learned things the hard way, perhaps from expensive experience. You've explained your concepts to clients dozens, perhaps hundreds of times. The problem is that those concepts have only lived in those conversations, meetings, phone calls, and Zooms when someone asks the right questions. Then, the conversation ends, and the brilliant insights disappear with it! The market never sees your brilliance! Which means the market has no reason to associate you with it.

The difference is rarely intelligence. The difference is documentation. One person has captured their thinking. The other has not. Until your thinking is documented, the market has no way to recognize you for the ideas you already carry. They cannot recognize expertise that has never been articulated. They cannot associate you with an idea that has never been named. Most experts are unknown because their best thinking has never been memorialized. And until that happens, the **Known-For Gap** remains wide open. Closing that gap is the real purpose of content. Content exists to capture your thinking so the market can recognize you for it.

To make matters worse, you may be using your industry's generic lingo and terms that don't specifically identify you. Even the Jersey Shore is doing better than you! Remember the phrase they coined "GTL" for Gym, Tan, Laundry? See, their simple daily ritual became an acronym that became a lifestyle mantra!

That's the **Known-For Gap.** You know things. But you're not known for them. And if you're honest, you've probably experienced this before. You explain something to a client, and they suddenly say, "Why have I never heard anyone explain it like that before?"

Or someone tells you, "You should really write a book about this." Or you walk away from a conversation thinking, "I've explained this same idea a hundred times." Those moments are clues that reveal something important...**You already have ideas worth sharing.**

Two professionals can have identical expertise, yet one appears to be the authority while the other remains invisible, mostly because one has made the common methods their own by explaining them in a novel way and using catchy, memorable, repeatable language. We will discuss your language and lingo in Part Two of this book.

BUSINESSES RUN ON COMMUNITY, NOT CLICK-BAIT

One of the biggest challenges about creator-type training is that they turn your focus on distracting metrics like views, likes, shares, and subscribers. This often causes you to lose sight of the ultimate goal: ensuring steady sales calls are booked, building a loyal customer base, and consistently closing deals. Shifting away from these tangible outcomes can leave you chasing numbers that, in reality, don't contribute directly to your business growth.

Modern creator-type training also focuses on growing your audience without context. Or showing you how to make clickbait. That is the equivalent of writing the word "SEX" at the top of an ad, only to say, *"Now that I've got your attention, let's talk about your life insurance!"* That flies like lead balloons. Once you've pissed off your reader, you lose them for life.

You may or may not be aware that followers, subscribers, or fans don't equal the power to sell anything. Yes, this is a really common mismatch: huge social numbers but almost no ability to move people in real life.

Why?

The creator-first economy gurus are teaching you to be algorithm-rich and real-world poor! Let's talk about passive vs. active fans. If you've gotten your following for the wrong reasons, most followers are passive scrollers, not people willing to buy tickets, drive across town, or rearrange a Friday night, let alone buy anything you're hawking.

You see examples of this everywhere. On TikTok, they're a god, but in real life, they can't fill a bus stop. They have tons of "reach," but nearly zero *bond* or habit with the audience. I don't even use the term *their* audience. Because, despite the number, do you consider them to really have an audience?

Real businesses run on continuity. They exist in the space between decisions. They survive on being remembered. They benefit from familiarity long before urgency appears. Most buying decisions aren't triggered by a single post or a perfectly timed message. They're the result of something quieter: repeated exposure to thinking that feels aligned, trustworthy, and relevant over time.

This is where standard creator-based thinking quietly fails business owners. Content, at its core, is how a business stays *present* in the minds of the people it serves. That presence doesn't require constant activity. It requires consistency of thought.

PREDICTABLE BEATS VIRAL EVERY TIME

Virality is intoxicating because it promises shortcuts:

One big post.
One big spike.
One moment of visibility that "changes" everything.

For most businesses, that moment never comes. And when it does, it rarely does what people hope. Spikes attract attention, not trust. They create curiosity, not readiness.

We know more now. In the beginning, it sounded like instant fame. There was a time that fame meant something. A movie star. A TV star. Now the internet has created famous people that nobody cares about. Most of them are famous for nothing but being who they are. It started with reality TV with folks like the Kardashians. That is just magnified with social media. Now, we know that fame is fleeting. The more "famous" people are being created, the more people roll their eyes. Research shows that the majority of viral moments amount to short-term buzz but no meaningful engagement. So, therefore, a waste of time and resources to chase. Especially when you can allocate those resources to effective content.

Trust, on the other hand, grows predictably. We consider it the "long game," but the long game can convert quickly. It grows when people see how you think, again and again. Maybe that annoying word "consistency" comes into play here. Your perspective feels familiar before they need it. Your standards are clear long before a conversation begins. People feel like you are like them, that you get them, and that you are for them.

This kind of trust doesn't look exciting from the outside. There are no fireworks. But over time, something important happens. The right people begin to recognize you. They remember you at the right moment. They reach out already pre-sold. That's content doing its real job.

CONTENT IS MEANT TO CLARIFY
AND DEMONSTRATE

One of the quiet burdens business owners carry is the feeling that content needs to convince people, change minds, and overcome objections. Buying happens when clarity replaces persuasion. Real buying decisions don't happen because someone was convinced. They happen because something finally became clear: clear that the problem is real, the timing is right, and that the person they're talking to understands their situation.

Content is meant to demonstrate your expertise. You shouldn't have to convince anyone of it. It's like Frank Sinatra with just a microphone and a spotlight. No special effects needed. You see the talent, no convincing necessary, just demonstration.

Content needs to meet your prospects where they already are. It needs to demonstrate that you know how they feel. When content clarifies and connects rather than convinces, resistance drops and decisions become easier. This is why aggressive content often backfires for business owners. It tries to manufacture urgency instead of respecting readiness, and readiness can't be rushed.

TIMING IS THE INVISIBLE VARIABLE
MOST CONTENT IGNORES

Every business owner has experienced this moment:

Someone reaches out and says, *"I've been following you for a while."* That sentence reveals something interesting. Why now? Why didn't they reach out the first time? The decision didn't happen in one moment. It happened in the background. Maybe it wasn't the right time. Perhaps they needed to get a few other things in line before they were ready. Maybe they needed to compare some other things. Either way, you snared them in your net, and you kept hold of them.

Timing is invisible. It can't be easily tracked because it varies for each buyer. But it's the single most important factor in buying behavior. Think of timing as the difference between a harvest and a hunt. A harvest requires patience and nurturing over time until everything is right, whereas a hunt is urgent and immediate. For your business, understanding this difference helps in nurturing potential buyers until they are ready to engage. Can someone trip on a piece of your content and say, "Oh, I've been wanting this!" and buy right away? Yes, that happens. The good news is that content can actually do both for you. Kill something to eat today, and plant seeds for a future harvest.

Most content advice ignores timing because it's inconvenient. But businesses that understand timing stop trying to force outcomes. They focus on being *available* when readiness appears. That's the real power of ongoing communication.

CONTENT AS A BUSINESS RESPONSIBILITY

For business owners, content isn't optional. Back in the 1900's, we used to create "content" in magazines, newspapers, and newsletters. We ran ads called "advertorials" that looked like articles to kinda fool people into thinking they were reading a magazine editorial or news coverage. This led to the TV version, called "infomercials." Infomercials are long-form TV programs, typically 30 minutes, broken into 3 parts that sell products. They connect with you on a "problem." They "agitate the problem." Then they show you the "solution" and demonstrate how their product solves your problem, peppering the presentation with "proof." All of this stuff was the "original" content marketing, and it's not far from what we should be doing with content today!

Okay, not many businesses, even in the Stone Age, did advertorials and infomercials, which explains why content marketing can feel like such a foreign idea to many today.

Therein lies your biggest opportunity! We used to have to pay for our advertorials, and now, with content marketing, you can post anywhere practically free, while your competition is STILL sleeping on it! To put this into perspective, a full-page advert in a popular magazine in the 1980s could easily run over $20,000. Today, the ability to reach thousands through digital platforms at no media cost means you can effectively advertise your business without the burden of such massive expenses.

Heck, if we were given FREE advertorials in magazines back in the day, who would have said *"No, thank you, I'm fine staying invisible!"*

Content is a responsibility. Not in the sense of obligation or pressure, but in the same way clarity is a responsibility. And refusing to accept free advertising opportunities takes a special kind of stupid. The ability to educate your perfect prospect is available essentially free now. You have the responsibility to yourself, your employees, and your market to clarify what you do and for whom you do it.

If people misunderstand what you do, if they don't recognize when you're relevant, or if they forget how you think, that's not the market's fault. Communication is how a business carries its perspective forward over time.

When content is treated as a hobby, it stays fragile. When it's treated as a performance, it becomes exhausting. When it's treated as a responsibility, it becomes stable. This stability is what most business owners are actually seeking.

WHY CONTENT RESISTANCE OFTEN MEANS YOU'RE OVERTHINKING

Many business owners describe themselves as "bad at content."

That's BS.

What they're actually bad at is ignoring the camera or microphone red light telling you it's recording. You're doing The Honeymooners' Ralph Kramden when he sees the camera's red light and freezes, sputtering, "Homina, homina, homina!" Ok, I just dated myself by about a century. (I'm not *that old*, I saw the black and white reruns as a kid!)

If you already sell a product or service by talking to people, whether in person or on the telephone, you're already doing content; it's just one-on-one. And you're probably good at it. All we are doing with content marketing is transcending time by canning and cloning your best presentation so it gets delivered at concert pitch every time. It's always ready and never calls in sick. Allowing people to self-serve or discover it when they want it—no appointment needed.

People resist content if they think they're putting on a show for a camera. They resist content that rewards theatrics over substance. They resist content that feels disconnected from the way they actually work. It takes a shift in context to alleviate that resistance, just like converting a movie to a stage play. Some things get adjusted. Your one-on-one sales presentations get converted to one-to-many. Just adjust and practice—no big deal.

CONTENT REFLECTS HOW YOU THINK, SO THE RIGHT PEOPLE CONNECT

Every piece of content, intentional or not, communicates something. It communicates your values, standards, priorities, judgment, and what and who you stand for and against.

Even silence communicates something.

This is where content becomes less about marketing and more about identity.

Especially today, as AI disrupts the world, you are being given a gift and an opportunity to stand out in a world of generic AI-created content. There's one thing that you should never neglect if you want to stand out:

Your perspective and unique edge.

People follow guides, sherpas, <u>Navigators</u>. They want a real person who can guide them past the bullshit. The one thing AI won't ever replace is your human perspective, voice, and personality. Today, the MESSENGER is more important than the MESSAGE, especially when the message is a commodity.

Show the world who "you" are, and your people will show up and reveal themselves. This is more about your personal (or professional) brand than marketing tactics.

THE BRIDGE YOU CAN'T SKIP

By now, something should feel settled. Content isn't about visibility for its own sake. It isn't about performing for algorithms (thank goodness!) It isn't about building an audience and hoping something happens later.

Effective content maintains clarity and distinction over time. That clarity has to come from somewhere. And it doesn't come from platforms, trends, or formulas. It comes from the part of your business that already works:

- ★ Your perspective
- ★ Your judgment
- ★ Your unique way of seeing problems and sequencing decisions.

In other words -- **YOUR MAGIC.**

Before content can compound, that magic has to be recognized, clarified, and captured. We want to capture your magic and turn what you know into what you want to be known *for*. This is an identity and branding exercise! And that's where we go next.

COMPLETING THE ARC OF PART ONE

Part One was designed to teach you how to remove the pressure to perform, name the misfit model you were resisting, and reframe content as something it should be. If this part felt relieving, that's intentional. The clarity you've gained makes execution possible.

Content exists to capture your thinking so the market can recognize you for it. And when your thinking becomes recognizable, something else begins to happen. Your content begins to produce something far more valuable than attention…It begins to produce cashflow.

But before your ideas can circulate in the world, they must first be captured, named, structured, and memorialized. That is where we turn next. Part Two is where the rubber meets the road. We'll start with recognizing what already works and learning how to memorialize it.

The problem isn't that you don't know enough. The problem is that the market doesn't know what you know.

KEY TAKEAWAYS

- The real content problem for most professionals is the **Known-For Gap**, the distance between what you know and what the market recognizes you for. Until your thinking is documented and named, the market has no way to associate you with your expertise.

- Content exists to support real business outcomes like clarity, trust, and readiness, not to chase attention, algorithms, or vanity metrics.

- Predictable, perspective-driven communication builds familiarity and trust faster than viral spikes ever could.

- Content works best when it demonstrates how you think and understand the buyer, rather than trying to persuade, hype, or force urgency.

- Timing can't be controlled, but a consistent presence ensures you are remembered when readiness appears.

- Treating content as a business responsibility stabilizes growth and allows your perspective to compound over time.

PART TWO

MEMORIALIZE YOUR MAGIC™

TURNING YOUR THINKING INTO AUTHORITY-BUILDING ASSETS

. . . .

"I saw the angel in the marble and carved until I set him free."

— MICHELANGELO

CHAPTER

THE MAGIC WITHIN

The Hidden Methods Behind Expert Thinking

....

"We know more than we can tell."
—MICHAEL POLANYI

....

Just last week on my book tour in Orlando, Florida, during a Q&A session, one of the 3,000+ in attendance asked me a great question. He asked, *"If I'm just getting started in business, what is the #1 most important thing to focus on to assure my success?"*

Great question, isn't it? My answer surprised many people there. It not only applies to those just getting started, but also to anyone who may be stuck or stalled in their business. My answer will also help anyone find the quickest path to success by avoiding time-wasting trial-and-error.

Here's my answer...

The number one problem I see plaguing most business owners and self-employed professionals, whether just getting started or

in business for years, is that they lack a clear message and a clear offer. So my advice is to focus on clarifying both.

In a nutshell, that is precisely what this entire section is about. And the first step is uncovering your clearest message, clarifying the problems you solve, and exactly who you help. Along with that message, you will define your process and give it a name that you can become known for.

The part about the offer…People need an easy way to engage with you, so you need an irresistible offer that needs no explanation.

Let's begin…

Well, it's pretty straightforward: *Name your method, watch your sales soar!* In this chapter, we'll explore ways to uncover *your* method and make it famous. When you can claim a system you created, and it's easy for the world to see clearly, your sales will skyrocket. People want a guide that has a plan. There's no better way to demonstrate that you have a plan than to give it a name and take ownership of your creation.

YOU NEED YOUR OWN LANGUAGE

Quick question…who "wrote the book" in your category? If you're in the financial field, would you say Dave Ramsey? If you're in personal development, would you say, "That's easy…Tony Robbins?" You see, their anchor in your mind is a book. They gave their magic a name and kept telling you about it. The anchor can be many things, like video or podcasts, but books are the apex asset. A book is like their collection of greatest hits.

These authors are not alone in their space. If I pressed you to name more, you could. Is Dave Ramsey the *only* financial topic author? Of course not. You may add Suze Orman or Ramit Sethi. So why not *you*? Why haven't *you* yet "written the book" in your field about *your* magic? Tony Robbins says that *"success leaves clues, yet few will notice until they're pointed out."*

Do you want more examples? Remember the P90X fitness commercials on TV? What was the name of the science that they claim to have created? Maybe it will jog your memory when I tell you that the creator of P90X, Tony Horton, called it "muscle confusion."

How about Shaun T from the same company with his fitness program called Insanity? Do you remember the name he gave to the science behind his program? He called it "max interval training."

By naming your intellectual property, you make it easier for the world to understand it as well as you do. You're giving your IP a nice wrapper with a ribbon and a bow.

Let me give you a couple more business examples to clarify this further…

- **Kaizen** – A Japanese term branded in the West as a continuous-improvement system used by companies and coaches as their "philosophy" or method.
- **EOS** (Entrepreneurial Operating System) – Gino Wickman's branded, structured system for running small businesses (Vision/Traction Organizer, Level 10 Meetings, etc.)
- **Inbound Marketing** – HubSpot's named methodology for attracting customers through content, search, and social instead of interruption advertising.

- **The 7 Habits System** – Stephen Covey's personal leadership framework, each "habit" forming part of a larger, named system.

- **Cashflow Content System** – Mark Imperial's signature method for turning everyday expertise into branded content that attracts clients, builds authority, and generates consistent revenue across platforms. You see what I did there?

Let me bring up something you may find weird. Cults. Let's stick to positive cults, not the nefarious ones. In business, utopia is essentially creating your own "cult" around *your* ideas and ideals. Something that cults all have is "language." They all have slang, shortcuts, and sayings that are unique to them. Bad cults like Heaven's Gate created language and terminology to manipulate. They portrayed Earth as a trap, referring to the unconverted as "lower forces," while considering their members as the enlightened "away team." The same anchor techniques they used for bad can be used for good.

In your content, whether in a book or on social posts, you will constantly plant *your language and expressions.* Let's look at some examples: The company Weight Watchers has language for their herd. "Points" are how they discuss the currency of food choices. "Zero-point foods," for example, are freebies that don't count toward daily allowances, allowing you to comply without guilt. CrossFit has insider language, like "WOD" for "Workout of the Day." Mary Kay Cosmetics uses "going for queen" as an aspirational expression that distributors use who aim to be top sellers. Orange Theory fitness calls its heart rate targets the "orange zone," which encapsulates the origins of their brand. What language can you create and memorialize in YOUR business?

You may be thinking, "Hey Mark, I'm a CPA and all CPAs do the same thing, and we all learn the same stuff in college, so how can I claim a system as my own?"

That's a great question! And here's the answer… just like you may have pancakes for breakfast and other people have a smoothie, even if there's one or two little things that you do differently or in your own way, that system becomes your own. Just claim it and own it.

Do you think Shaun T was the first person to do high-intensity interval training? He shows you *his* approach, and he calls it "max interval training." Was Beto Perez the first person to teach Latin dance as a fitness regimen? Of course not, but he was the first person to create his own formula and give it a name, Zumba, and now he's known as the creator of a multi-billion dollar business.

Think about it this way….lots of people play the guitar, but Jimi Hendrix was unmistakable. Having a personal flair in execution wins loyalty. If you're a lawyer, you can win cases, and if you claim a one-of-a-kind method, or a "3-step justice framework," you'll win trust.

I hope by now I've made my point and you are ready to claim your magic! Now let's talk about how to unpack your magic.

As I pointed out at the end of the previous chapter, you are already a content creator, only under the radar. If you deal with customers in your store or prospects over the phone, you are already sharing and demonstrating your unique wisdom and abilities. You're telling them how you feel about approaching their problem. You're showing them empathy by understanding their feelings and experiences because you've been in their shoes. You're demonstrating how your solution stands out from others they may have tried. You make them believe you can finally help them, even though nothing else has worked.

When you're working with your prospects and customers in person or on the phone, you're likely focused on their problem and helping them. You're answering their questions and pointing out what they should ask, but because they don't know enough, they don't ask. This is the same stuff you should talk about when you make content.

Every day, I speak with many aspiring authors who are confused about what to write about. They'll even say, *"I have no idea what I should write."* I help them get past that block by asking them, "If you could wave a magic wand and you'd be guaranteed success in getting anything you wanted from your book, what would that be? How do you define success?" Many will tell me that they want the instant credibility and authority that being an author gives you. Others will say they want to attract all the clients they ever wanted and to pursue other opportunities to meet prospects by speaking at events or appearing as a guest on other people's podcasts. Now we're getting somewhere.

Then I ask, "If attracting unlimited clients, speaking opportunities, and podcast opportunities were utopia, what would we have to show those people that would draw them to you like a magnet?" It's kind of a rhetorical question, but they'll say, *"Well, I'll have to give them something they already want, like a solution to one of their problems."* Ok, perfect. What's that specific, bleeding-neck problem that keeps them up at night, such as "lacking cash flow" or "stagnant growth," that your book solves? Now we're heading down the path that will inform the book's appeal and title. It should also be something that you want to be known for.

When you can memorialize your perspective into a signature book, you have a powerful, lifelong apex asset that will do a lot of heavy lifting and make attracting clients a whole lot easier.

This is the same thinking you need for your content. I call it **"memorializing your magic."** Your magic is your unique edge in how you see the world and how you work to solve your clients' problems.

By the time business owners start thinking seriously about content, most of them assume they're missing something; perhaps more confidence, clarity, originality, or personality. They look around and see people who seem more articulate, more visible, and more comfortable sharing ideas publicly, and quietly conclude that content success must belong to a certain type of person. That assumption is wrong. And it's one of the most damaging beliefs business owners carry into content because it puts the focus in the wrong area. Sure, confidence, clarity, and personality have a place. And the good news is that you will get better and better every day you put in the reps, so don't worry.

PERSPECTIVE IS THE DIFFERENTIATOR

Most professionals underestimate how much they already know. Not because they lack skill, but because familiarity dulls value. What feels obvious to you often feels profound to someone encountering it for the first time. What feels routine to you is often the result of years of judgment, trial, and sequencing decisions correctly. But expertise alone isn't what creates resonance. You need perspective! Perspective is how you see problems, how you prioritize, and how you decide what matters first and what can wait.

Two experts can know the same facts and still sound completely different. One clarifies. The other confuses. The weird part is that both types will find an audience. That difference is judgment, and it's where your magic lives!

The notes already existed before Beethoven came along. The English language already existed before the poets came along. It's all about arrangement.

THE PATTERN HIDING INSIDE
YOUR BEST WORK

If you look closely at the work you're most proud of, the clients who got the best results, the projects that felt aligned, and the conversations that flowed easily, you'll notice something. You were applying a pattern. Something you've done instinctually all along. It's how you naturally applied your knowledge and experience.

You asked certain questions first. You noticed certain signals early. You avoided certain mistakes instinctively. That pattern came from experience. And over time, it became automatic. That's why it feels invisible to you now.

Magic rarely looks magical from the inside. It looks obvious.

WHY PEOPLE RESONATE
WITH HOW YOU THINK

"People may hear your words, but they feel your attitude."
—John C. Maxwell, Author

When people say they're drawn to someone's content, they rarely mean the information itself. They mean the *way* it's framed. The order ideas are presented. The assumptions that are challenged. The things that are emphasized (or ignored).

People follow thought patterns and stories. Stories have a point. They have a logic. So people are automatically listening for alignment with someone who sees the problem the way they do, or articulates it better than they ever could. I always say, *"If you can describe someone's problem better than they can, you will capture their attention!"*

That's why two people can say the same thing and get completely different responses. One sounds generic, while the other sounds unmistakable. Your voice is your personal and professional brand.

THE MAGIC OF BEING MORE
PROLIFIC THAN PERSONALITY

One of the quiet pressures of modern content is the belief that personality is the point.

Be louder! Be more expressive! Be more visible!

But personality doesn't build trust. Consistency does. There's that goofy word again, but let's put it in the right context. I'm not saying be consistent just for the sake of showing up all the time. I'm talking about consistently singing the same hit songs like you're Taylor Swift. You then become familiar over time to the point where an increasing herd of people says, *"Oh, there's so and so, the [widget] guy."* This is where you start to become known.

It is reassuring for your audience when they see consistency in how you think, what you prioritize, and what you won't compromise. And reassurance is what people seek when decisions matter. The best news is that your topic likely yields lots of things people want to know and need to know.

The most trusted professionals aren't practiced entertainers. My main mentor and one of the biggest names in the marketing field, Dan Kennedy, exemplifies this idea through his focus on substance over polish. Despite having to overcome a stutter and frequently using 'um' in his speech, his influence and success aren't hindered by these perceived imperfections. Instead, they highlight that what truly matters is the depth and consistency of his message. His listeners resonate with his reliability and content, proving that authenticity and substance can surpass flawlessness. They even mimic him, seeing beyond the words to the valuable insights he shares.

I want to adjust your focus on being more *prolific* with your consistent message. Don't worry so much about your voice. Just put in the reps. Your voice will come out over time. And people will appreciate that you are a real person.

WHY YOUR MAGIC FEELS
HARD TO ARTICULATE

If this all sounds true, but still feels frustrating, you're not alone. Most business owners struggle to articulate their magic because they're too close to it, like the goldfish that can't see the water inside the bowl.

You've internalized your thinking. You've been doing things so instinctually that you've never had to explain things to anyone. You've stopped noticing the decisions you make automatically. You forget that people don't know your subject as well as you do. And that gap, the distance between how you think and how others struggle, is where your value lives. But it requires slowing down enough to notice it, which is uncomfortable.

I'll give you an example. In my signature book service, I help professionals turn what they know into what they want to be known for. The funny thing is, they think that they are writing a book, and I always point out that the reality is *the book* will be writing *them*!

What do I mean by that?

Likely, they've never taught anyone their process. They operate on instincts and have never documented their own thinking process. Writing the book is forcing them to transfer their thinking to others, and that is life-changing, not just for the reader, but for the author!

I've been a lifelong martial artist, and over the years, to achieve my black belt, I was required to train others below my rank. As an adult,

I see now that it sharpened me. It forced me to master my technique if I had to teach it to others. That's what writing your book is going to do, and it will change your life. Creating content works in the same way. The content is going to create *you*.

CONTENT FAILS WHEN
IDENTITY IS UNCLEAR

When I first started speaking, I had no idea what I was doing. Heck, sometimes I'm still nervous to speak, and I've been doing this for two decades. A black belt in martial arts is just a white belt that never quit. That's how I look at it, and forever I will be a student.

I started speaking by watching other speakers and just copying what they did. "Fake it till you make it" is the expression. I didn't find my own voice until I really discovered my capabilities. Confidence comes from capabilities. So always be moving, but you can certainly benefit and do better than I by doing some basic work on defining your own identity.

Many people jump straight to execution without clarifying identity. I did it myself at first. They borrow formats. They mimic voices. They follow frameworks. And while those tools may work temporarily, they never quite feel right because they're expressing someone else's thinking. When I did it, I felt like I was wearing someone else's clothes. Content built on borrowed identity always feels fragile. It requires constant effort, validation, and adjustment. Content built on a clarified identity only needs to be true.

YOU DON'T NEED IDEAS, YOU NEED RECOGNITION

One of the most freeing realizations business owners have is this: You don't need to invent anything. You need to clarify and claim what you already have. You need to put it out in the world in a way people can easily wrap their minds around and anchor your concepts to you. You need recognition. You need to become *known*.

Recognition of:

- What you already do well
- How you already think
- Why people already trust you

Known for:

- What you stand for
- Who you stand for
- What you stand against
- What you do for whom you help
- How you do what you do

The raw material for your content already exists in your conversations and in your "let me explain this a different way" moments.

WHY THIS CHAPTER COMES BEFORE ANY FRAMEWORK

It's tempting to move quickly here. You might be eager to jump into structure, name steps, and introduce systems. But before we dive into frameworks, imagine a future where your content effortlessly captures your audience's attention, satisfying their needs before they even realize what they want. This is just a glimpse of the transformative power the upcoming structure will unlock.

Before content can compound, it has to be grounded. Before execution can feel calm, identity has to feel clear. I'm not asking you to *do* anything yet. All I'm asking is for you to take notice, observe how you already think, pay attention to where people consistently respond, and recognize patterns you've been overlooking.

Once you see your magic clearly, capturing it becomes natural.

And that's what we'll do next.

THE SHIFT THAT MAKES EVERYTHING EASIER

There's a subtle moment when business owners stop trying to "be good at content" and begin recognizing themselves in it. They stop asking, *"What should I say?"* And start asking: *What do I already say that works?*

That shift changes everything. It turns content from something you produce into something you preserve.

In the next chapter, we're going to dismantle the myth of the guru. We're going to talk about authority without performance. About curation instead of invention. About why your job isn't to create new notes, it's to arrange them your way.

Because the notes were already there long before Beethoven ever picked up a pen.

KEY TAKEAWAYS

- You do not need new ideas. You need to recognize, name, and claim the pattern you already apply instinctively in your best work.

- Perspective is the differentiator. The facts may be shared by many, but your judgment, sequencing, and emphasis are what make you unmistakable.

- When you describe someone's problem better than they can, you capture their heart and earn their trust.

- Consistency in how you think builds reassurance, and reassurance is what people seek when decisions matter.

- Before you reach for frameworks or tactics, get clear on identity. Once you see your magic clearly, capturing and compounding it becomes natural.

CHAPTER

THERE ARE NO GURUS, ONLY CURATORS

*Why Authority Comes From How
You Organize Ideas*

....

"The notes were already there before Beethoven came along."

– MARK IMPERIAL

....

Let me say something that might sound a bit controversial at first. There are no gurus. Not in the way most people think. Most of the people you look up to, follow, and learn from didn't wake up one day with completely original ideas. They didn't invent wisdom out of thin air. What they've done, whether they realize it or not, is learned, observed, tested, and most importantly, organized what works. They became known not because they created something entirely new, but because they made ideas clear, usable, and repeatable for others. In other words, **they curated.** I see myself as a curator. Do I have some original thoughts? Of course, however, they're based around something I've learned, observed, and either agreed with or not. That makes what I say about it original.

Somewhere along the way, we were sold the idea that authority belongs only to inventors; real leaders come up with new ideas, build frameworks from scratch, and earn respect by saying things no one has ever said. This belief is a double-edged sword. On one edge, it convinces you there's no room for you. It makes you think that the space is crowded and experts are already established. You're late to the party.

On the other edge, it's a massive advantage because that same belief is quietly stopping your competitors too! Let's keep that our little secret so we have less competition.

What looks like competition is simply activity without architecture. People posting without doctrine and talking without judgment. When you learn to memorialize your magic with structure, you're no longer competing with noise. Noise is loud. Structure is rare. Rare wins, and clarity always outperforms volume.

Once authority is framed as invention, content becomes a performance, and most professionals instinctively resist that role. Not because they lack ideas but because they recognize the absurdity of pretending they invented gravity. You're not going to do that. You're the one who makes gravity better.

Most people are waiting to feel qualified. They're waiting to feel original. They're waiting to feel like a "guru." That's the real misconception. There are no gurus. There are only curators who have the courage to arrange what they've learned, claim their perspective, and speak clearly. Every so-called guru built their authority the same way you will by organizing ideas that already existed, filtering them through experience, and presenting them with conviction. They didn't invent truth; they arranged it.

Instead of standing outside, looking up at a mountaintop crowded with "gurus," you need to realize that you are already among them. Before: *"Those experts are leagues ahead, and I need a breakthrough to join them."* After: *"I'm already here, arranging and sharing ideas with my unique perspective just like they did."*

The moment you understand that, the hierarchy collapses. And you realize we are all "gurus."
You stop asking, *"Who am I to say this?"* And you start asking, *"Why wouldn't I?"*

THE PRESSURE TO BE ORIGINAL

Originality is a highly misunderstood concept in modern business culture. It's constantly praised and superficially rewarded, so that's why people chase it. Yet the pioneers returned with arrows in their backs. Invention is overrated.

Almost none of the ideas that shape our world are truly new. They're refinements. translations, and innovations. Business owners begin avoiding ideas that feel "obvious," even when those ideas are precisely what their audience needs to hear. They hesitate to repeat principles that matter, which is how content loses its grounding.

AUTHORITY HAS ALWAYS BEEN
ABOUT SELECTION, NOT CREATION

"Absorb what is useful. Discard what is not.
Add what is uniquely your own."
—Bruce Lee

Long before anyone talked about personal brands or thought leadership, authority worked differently. The most influential figures in history were "selectors." They chose which ideas mattered. They emphasized certain principles over others. And they arranged existing knowledge into usable order.

They worked in a lot of ways, like a disc jockey. Disc jockeys are selectors. They assemble their own unique order of "the best" selections. They have their own style in packing a dancefloor. Some start slow and peak fast. Some throw in left turns to make people cheer. Some DJs are known for being eclectic and obscure, while others play bangers. You see, you have the power to choose how you want to be known. DJs are record "selectors." You are a methodology "selector."

A person who consistently chooses the right ideas earns authority without ever claiming genius. This is what curators do to differentiate themselves from "gurus." The word "guru" carries weight, and not the good kind. It implies "better than others." Most business owners aspire to build trusted partnerships with their clients. Rather than seeking followers, they focus on building relationships rooted in mutual respect and understanding. "Thought leadership" often feels misaligned because it asks professionals to adopt a persona they never sought. Curation shifts the goal from being impressive to being useful.

THE BEETHOVEN PROBLEM

Are you worried about being accused of stealing someone else's ideas? About not being original?

I always say, *"The notes were already there before Beethoven came along."* I want to permit you to re-arrange the notes, just as Beethoven did. Just like any "guru" does, frankly.

Before Beethoven composed, the notes already existed. He didn't invent music. He selected combinations that expressed something that felt inevitable once heard. No one accused him of stealing notes because the value was never in the notes themselves. It was in what he did with them.

The same is true for business ideas. Frameworks, principles, and language existed before you. Your authority comes from how you assemble them (and tell the world about them). When you take how YOU do things, even if they're a combination of things you've learned from twenty other sources, and put them together into a NEW, curated order, they are now YOURS. **Frame it. Name it. Make it famous.**

TRANSLATION IS MORE VALUABLE
THAN ORIGINALITY

Several people can share the same idea, but it's the person who expresses it most memorably, whether through creativity, clarity, or simplicity, who stands out. The difference between being overlooked and becoming well-known often comes down to phrasing, tone, and timing. A clever turn of phrase, a metaphor that instantly clicks, or a statement that feels effortlessly relatable can make an ordinary idea unforgettable. In a world flooded with similar messages, those who say it best aren't necessarily the most original, but they're the most clear, the most catchy, and the most shareable.

If you're the one who takes a complex concept and makes it simple for people to wrap their heads around, then you wrap it in an easy-to-repeat, maybe even catchy name, you have a higher chance at gaining KVT. You've heard of KLT (Know-Like-Trust). I aim for KVT (Know-VALUE-Trust). When someone values you, they not only like you but also deem you important in their life. If you want clients, you don't want just to be liked; you want to be valued and respected.

Gary Keller wrote the book "The One Thing," and it caught fire. His concept was basic, and anyone could have said it. The concept was "What's the ONE thing holding you back? Do that first, everything else is noise." While productivity gurus preached multi-tasking myths, Keller boiled his message down to "The One Thing," and this question-plus-command turned overwhelming to-do lists into a single, magnetic daily ritual for real estate moguls and entrepreneurs, outshining 500-page planners. The book has sold over 2 million copies and topped the Wall Street Journal bestseller list. See how he showed people a "better way," and the world ate it up?

The 1998 book "Who Moved My Cheese?" disrupted the noise of navigating business or life. While management consultants were babbling about adaptability frameworks, Johnson boiled it down to a 94-page parable about mice and "little people" racing after new cheese with the core phrase "Cheese moves. Get over it and find more." This cheesy (pun intended) concept sold 28 million copies and is still being quoted by corporate trainers today over dry SWOT analyses. How crazy is that? What's YOUR version of "Who Moved My Cheese?"

Author Mel Robbins simplified the complex topic of detaching from others' drama, opinions, and outcomes to protect your own energy. If people ghost you, she says, "Let them." If people judge you, she says, "Let them." This topic has been covered many times by other people using $1 words. When Mel Robbins distilled her message into her uber-simple book title, "Let Them," it was like a permission slip or a pressure relief valve for the world. So much so, people are getting "Let Them" tattoos! That's the power of your language and your translation.

When you translate ideas through your own real-world insights and judgment, you add value even when the ideas themselves may be unremarkable on the surface, especially when they're familiar!

BORROWING FRAMEWORKS BUILDS TRUST (WHEN DONE CORRECTLY)

I just shared with you how you will be curating your own frameworks from how you do things. Are there some frameworks you use in your work that come from others? That's totally okay! As long as you credit the creator! In fact, it builds even more trust when you share a framework saying, *"Here's something I learned from _____ that has always served me well..."*

You are signaling several things at once. One, you are always learning, and school is never out for the pro. Two, you are humble and do not need to take credit for "everything" you know. Three, you will be signaling to the creator (and the world) that you are one of the good guys. This can put you in those creators' radars and in the hearts of your audience.

CURATION REQUIRES MORE RESPONSIBILITY THAN CREATION

Curation forces consistency (there's that word again), and consistency builds recognition over time. This is good news because it means that you don't always have to be seeking something new to share. You will be finding a finite number of drums to beat, and you will be beating those drums forever in different ways.

This is why curated content often feels calmer. A mentor I studied often was Gary Halbert, and he had an expression, *"You only have so many clicks on the dial."* What he meant was that, no matter the topic or challenge, different people will solve it through their own filter. If someone asked Gary's group of experts how they could grow their business, you could expect the event expert to talk about using live events. The direct mail guy would explain how to do a mailing campaign, and the online expert would teach how to build a funnel.

The goal of your curation is to choose the one big problem that your business or service solves. I'm sure there are multiple ways in your service to solve that one big problem. Those are your clicks on the dial. You will master those, frame them, name them, and make them magic. Your responsibility is to keep the focus on the one big problem.

At this point, your identity as a Business Owner Creator should feel clearer. You're not a creator chasing attention. You're also not a guru claiming authority. You're a business owner who curates thinking responsibly so you can help others make better decisions. This is something you already practice daily. Now that you understand this role, you can move into action.

In the next chapter, we'll name what this process actually is. We'll talk about what it means to **"memorialize your magic"** as a practical way to capture judgment before it disappears. The goal isn't to turn you into a louder, 'guru-type,' but to make what already works last longer.

Magic captured compounds. Imagine this momentum like a flywheel gaining speed with every turn. Each insight you memorialize adds another push, making what you build harder to stop and easier to move forward. Let this mantra and mental image guide you as you move ahead.

KEY TAKEAWAYS

- Authority is earned by arranging and claiming ideas with conviction, not by pretending you invented them.

- What looks like competition is usually noise without structure, and structure is what wins.

- You do not need to be a guru to lead; you need the courage to curate what you know and speak clearly.

- The clearest translator of an idea often becomes more valuable than the most original thinker.

- Focus on the one big problem you solve, master your clicks on the dial, and let consistency compound your magic.

HOW TO MEMORIALIZE YOUR MAGIC

Captured Ideas Becomes Doctrine
You're "Known-For"

....

"Raw talent is invisible until captured.
Frame it, name it, and make it magic."

—MARK IMPERIAL

....

Ideas come and go every day. The ones that matter get memorialized. Publishing is just putting something out there, but memorializing means capturing and documenting it. When you memorialize something, you're saying it matters enough to last. We memorialize events because they shaped us. We memorialize people because they influenced us. We memorialize ideas because they deserve continuity.

Many business owners lose their best ideas, not because they aren't valuable, but because they never write them down. Wouldn't you want a "greatest hits" collection of your best work? People love greatest hits. That's how they know their favorite artists. You're no different. You're the business equivalent of Taylor Swift. Ok, maybe the Police. Ever heard of a concert where the artist only performed their unknown, unreleased, or B-sides? They get bad reviews because people went there for a reason. I tell my DJ students this all the time. Don't play obscure versions at a party just to be "cool." The people like those songs for a reason, give them the version they know, not some remix.

No matter how you see it, your job is to 1) figure out your "hits," 2) keep sharing your greatest hits, and 3) occasionally come up with something new, often just a fresh take on one of your existing hits. Your hits will live in conversations, explanations, and off-the-cuff corrections. In "let me explain this a different way" moments. When you memorialize your magic, you help your market remember your expertise and judgment.

WHY MAGIC MUST BE CAPTURED BEFORE IT CAN COMPOUND

Things can't grow or build up over time unless you preserve them. Money compounds because it stays invested. Trust compounds because it stays consistent. Brands compound because their meaning doesn't change every month. If you don't capture your magic, it can't build up. It just disappears. That's why many smart business owners always feel busy but never ahead. They're generating value but not storing it. Every explanation is said differently. Every clarification is temporary. Every insight disappears after the conversation ends.

Cashflow Content isn't about making you a publisher or merely a content creator. It's about turning your best ideas into valuable assets. To do that, you need a framework. Let's explore your unique strengths so you can define them, give them a name, and make them well-known. We'll use my **M.A.G.I.C. Identity Framework**™ for this. Treat it like a workshop; grab a notepad and start writing down your answers.

THE M.A.G.I.C. IDENTITY FRAMEWORK™

The **M.A.G.I.C. Identity Framework**™ helps you clarify and capture what makes your thinking unique, so it shows up naturally and consistently. At the highest level:

M.A.G.I.C. is the process of turning judgment into doctrine. Let's begin...

M.A.G.I.C.

- **M — MISSION**
- **A — ARTICULATE**
- **G — GRID**
- **I — INTEGRATE**
- **C — CLAIM**

M — MASTER YOUR MISSION

Many business owners believe their problem is with content, but it's really about mission. They think they simply have to be consistent, choose the right platform, or figure out what to post. So they try different trends, copy formats, and imitate others.

Cashflow comes from being clear rather than creative. If your mission isn't clear, your content lacks focus. If it's weak or broad, your message won't stick or attract attention. Before we discuss things like timing, audience awareness, or distribution, we need to set a clear direction for your mission by answering one key question:

Why should this person, at this moment, care?

When your mission is clear, three things happen immediately:

1. You recognize your ideal client faster, and they recognize you.
2. You repel the wrong people without drama.
3. You know exactly what questions to answer in your content.

You'll stop guessing, posting randomly, or sharing "value content" that feels useful but doesn't get results. A clear mission keeps you focused, and that focus is what drives cashflow. When people are confused, they don't take action.

This is where *Memorialize Your Magic* actually begins. Your magic lies in connecting with your ideal tribe by entering the conversation already in their minds. Your magic signals that you have something they want and that they may never have seen anywhere else. If you can't explain your magic clearly, it stays in your head and your market can't reward what they don't understand. Clarity helps people see your value. When your mission is clear, making decisions is easier, and your content becomes more focused. Conversations are shorter, and prospects either connect with your message or they don't.

Here are the main questions you should answer for yourself. These will guide the content you create:

- WHAT BIG PROBLEM DO YOU SOLVE? (Zoom out)
- FOR *WHOM* DO YOU SOLVE IT? (Be as specific as possible)
- WHAT DOES IT COST THEM IF THEY IGNORE IT? (Time/money/lifestyle)
- WHAT FALSE BELIEF ARE YOU CORRECTING?
- WHAT TRANSFORMATION DO YOU DELIVER? (Who will they become?)
- WHY ARE YOU UNIQUELY EQUIPPED TO SOLVE THE PROBLEM? (What qualifies you beyond your education?)
- WHO IS THIS *NOT* FOR? (It's just as important to turn away the wrong people as it is to attract the right ones.)
- WHAT PRINCIPLE ARE YOU WILLING TO DEFEND? (People are drawn to those who stand for something)

The Mission Declaration

To make this clear, fill in the blanks below. Keep your answers short and focused.

I serve _____
who are stuck with _____.
Most of them believe _____.
If they don't fix it, it costs them _____.
I help them become _____.
This is not for _____.

If you can't fill out those six lines without losing focus, you just have a list of options, not a mission. If your mission isn't clear, your magic goes unnoticed and your market doesn't respond. If you found it hard to complete that declaration, that's actually a good thing because the struggle is helpful.

Most professionals operate with a general intention, not a defined mission. They want to help. They want to serve and add value. But markets respond to clear results, not just good intentions. When your mission is clear, you focus on the changes you create, not just the tasks you do.

But here's where many business owners misstep: they think a mission is enough. Knowing your destination is important, but if you can't explain the path, people won't follow. A clear mission gets attention; a clear process builds trust. Your mission says, *"This is who I help and what I solve."* Your process says, *"Here's how I solve it."* That's when your magic becomes visible, and that's what we'll cover next.

A — ARTICULATE YOUR PROCESS

"The limits of my language mean the limits of my world."
—Ludwig Wittgenstein

Turn Invisible Instinct Into Visible Doctrine

Most professionals are capable, but very few are articulate. Swipe right on that because that is the core reason this book exists. You will have the edge because I just put a giant spotlight on what most professionals and business owners need to focus on. Now you are at an advantage if you take action on what you are learning here.

You already have a way of doing things. You already make decisions in a particular order. You already reject certain approaches instinctively. But if you cannot explain your thinking clearly, it looks like experience instead of method. Experience earns respect while method earns authority. Articulation is where your invisible instinct becomes visible doctrine. It is the moment your magic stops being private and starts becoming repeatable.

Step One: Study the Default

Before you define your difference, you must define the norm. This isn't talking about you. This is talking about how things are. How does everyone else in your industry typically operate? What advice gets repeated endlessly? What assumptions go unchallenged? What does the average competitor emphasize? Your authority begins with contrast.

Start by articulating the default, then articulate your distinction. Complete this sentence:

"In my industry, most people focus on _____. I focus on _____."

Keep refining your answer until it doesn't sound "soft." Clarity here sharpens positioning instantly.

Step Two: Declare Your Doctrine

Now we move from contrast to conviction. Where do you disagree? What do you refuse to do? What common advice do you believe is incomplete or misapplied? What principle guides your decisions consistently?

Every strong brand has a doctrine, and this isn't just an opinion. And it shouldn't sound reactionary or attacking anything; it should sound like a statement.

Doctrine sounds like:

- *"Content exists to drive action, not applause."*
- *"Answers move decisions more than information."*
- *"Clarity compounds faster than volume."*

Doctrine acts as a filter for everything you create. It shapes your content, anchors your messaging, and signals intentionality. This is where you signal to the world what you stand for.

Step Three: Name Your Things

In Chapter Four, I told you that you needed your own language. Your language begins with how you name your ideas and concepts to make them stand out and be memorable. Authority benefits from pattern recognition. That's how you memorize the lyrics of your favorite songs without even consciously thinking about it. There's that music and greatest hits reference again!

What are the "big pieces" of your puzzle? Start with the big problem that you solve. What are the three to five big things your market needs to solve that big problem? Take inventory of those things and give them YOUR OWN NAME.

Call them something...

Three phases...
Five pillars...
Four levers...

I'll give you an example from my own brand. If you were to look at what "I" am about, it starts here...

→ **THE BIG PROBLEM I SOLVE:** Standing out in a crowded field. How to not be invisible.
→ **WHOM I SOLVE THIS FOR:** Business owners and self-employed professionals
→ **WHAT ARE THE "BIG PILLARS" OF THE PUZZLE:** Positioning - Branding - Marketing - Sales

I have my own view of those pillars. And I am keenly aware of how the world "sees" those pillars. Therefore, it informs how I speak about each of them so my points land.

I've given those pillars unique names:

BRANDING/MARKETING - I call my methodology **ActionBrand™ Marketing**, my own doctrine that emerged from years of watching the two disciplines, branding and marketing, treated separately, with fans of one side or the other, when in reality they both need to coexist to succeed.

SALES - I have a brand called **"Selling for the People."** My focus is on everyday professionals who excel in their work and dislike self-promotion. Unlike most sales training, which targets elite, high-ticket experts seeking incremental gains, I serve those who prefer client work over prospecting and selling.

Did you notice that I bundled branding and marketing in one? For me, this is intentional because my doctrine expresses that the two are not mutually exclusive. And that branding cannot exist without marketing. And that you don't own your brand, it is owned in the mind of your market. And we don't build a brand to get a customer, but get a customer to build a brand.

Also, note that I don't lead with much talk about the concept of "positioning." Although positioning is the most crucial piece of the puzzle, few people wake up thinking they *need* positioning. Positioning is the spine on which branding is built, so I bake it into my branding pillar since that is what people "think" they need. Sell them what they want, but give them what they need. That's why we put cheese on broccoli.

Can you see all the things happening here?

Even if reality is complex, articulation demands structure. We will unpack this in the next pillar **"G"** of the M.A.G.I.C framework. When you find your big pillars and create your own frameworks around the solution to those pillars, you're on your way to becoming legendary.

The Napkin Test

Explain your process in five steps or fewer. If it does not fit on a napkin, it will not fit in someone's memory. You are not oversimplifying; you are organizing, and the organization develops trust.

Pro Tip: Dissect Your Own Sales Conversation

If you're having trouble identifying the big pillars of your process or the steps you take to help your clients, look at your existing sales conversations. Your articulation is already happening. Listen carefully to your sales calls. What question does a client ask right before they commit? What fear must be calmed? What belief must shift? What misconception must be corrected? When you extract those patterns and address them consistently in your content, you stop "sharing knowledge" and start removing decision friction.

Step Four: Define Your Language

Remember, in Chapter Four, I said you need your own language. This is the step where you begin to catalog your language. You only need a starter set of language because this is a lifelong journey. New concepts and new expressions will come to you all the time. Your language will evolve, so don't be afraid of it. Just set up some starting blocks.

In the previous step, you named your big pillars. In this step, I want you to drill down deeper and perhaps start giving elements of your process a language. When you work with a client, is there a before-and-after picture that you can define or give a name? You don't have to name everything, but this is just an idea. For example, dating coaches often described the before picture, or in other words, an untrained, struggling person in dating, by naming them an AFC or "average frustrated chump." Not too flattering, I know, but it got the point across, and that became a memorable acronym that the dating world instantly recognized. I don't remember where I first heard that term, and I'm not going to Google it. Perhaps you can look it up. But that term became part of that person's language.

Can you give the challenge that people are going through a name? Or the problem you help them solve? The author Mike Michalowicz described what he was against as "entrepreneurial poverty."

What do you call the enemy? In Dan Kennedy's time management book, he referred to the enemy, which are people or things that waste your time, as "time vampires."

You could look at the same eight elements in the previous pillar **"M,"** and be inspired to come up with your own names for them.

Language creates identity. Pay attention to the words you repeat naturally. The metaphors you use. The phrases you prefer. The terms you refuse to adopt because "anti-whatever" can inspire language. When you name ideas, you create ownership. When you consistently mention those names, you create recall. Distinct language separates you from generic positioning. If your vocabulary sounds identical to your competitors', your positioning will feel identical too.

Step Five: Extract Your Decision Framework

This is what separates the wise masters from the mediocre majority. Most professionals can describe what they do. Few can describe how they decide. Most operate on instincts and ignore the value of articulating their moves to the world.

When there are many ways to be right, how do you choose? What criteria matter most? That decision logic is your real intellectual property. It cannot be copied easily because it is built on judgment. When you articulate how you think, not just what you do, you move from practitioner to strategist. And strategists command trust faster.

Articulation is the difference between *"I've been doing this for twenty years,"* and *"Here is the system I use."* The first earns admiration. The second earns authority. Once articulated, your process can be structured, diagrammed, repeated, integrated, and claimed.

Without articulation, your magic stays trapped in your head. With articulation, it becomes doctrine. And doctrine is what allows someone else to follow the path. Which is why articulation is not the end, but the raw materials. Because once your thinking is clear, it must become visible. That is where **G** begins.

G — GRID YOUR STEPS

If **M** earns attention and **A** reframes belief, then **G** must reduce confusion and give clarity to your way of thinking. Generate your grid.

To make instant oatmeal, the instructions say:

1. Empty the packet into the bowl.
2. Add ½ cup hot water or milk.
3. Stir and let stand for 1 minute.

There's a reassurance in knowing what to expect. Same for your work and for comforting your prospects by letting them know what to expect with your process. Authority is shown by how clearly you can reveal the path. This is where you reduce everything into phases they can see and steps they can follow. Three to five big movements. Three to five clear actions inside each. No complexity for the sake of looking intelligent. When you map the journey using a grid, a ladder, a matrix, or a simple arc, you signal structure. Structure is rare, and rare is valuable.

"But wait, Mark, there are 30 micro-steps here!" That's okay, you don't have to major in the minor things. Just show the "one big thing" those 30 micro-steps accomplish, and we can suppress the minutia.

If someone can see where they are, where they're going, and the next step to take, you've already differentiated yourself from the noise.

G is where you turn perspective into process, sequence, and turn "That makes sense" into "I know what to do next!" Without **G**, content feels smart. With **G**, content feels safe. And safety moves decisions.

The Magic in the Matrix

I prefer 3 "phases" or "pillars" simply because humans easily understand things in threes. That's why we have "lather-rinse-repeat," "stop-drop-roll," "ready-set-go," "dream-believe-achieve," "Blood-sweat-tears," "faster-better-cheaper," "life-liberty-happiness," "past-present-future," and on and on. Ok, I'll stop. And if I have 3 steps within each of the 3, then I have a 3x3 matrix. Easy.

Are you familiar with the term "UX" (User Experience)? For example, with software or electronics, people are drawn to the "easy." When software is first created, often the number of operations or steps can be daunting. It is the job of UX designers to dumb down or simplify the software's look and feel to make it approachable and usable for the operator. Easy is hard to spell! The job is to take your work, no matter how complex or simple, and make it *appear* easy.

I heard a speaker say, *"If you give me all day to teach a topic, I don't need any preparation. If I only have an hour, I'll need a week to prepare."* In 1657, Blaise Pascal wrote, *"I have only made this letter longer because I have not had the time to make it shorter."*

This is the work! And no one of your competitors has done it! So take advantage!

Here's how you could look at your matrix…

1. Phases (The Rocks in the Pond)

These are the big pillars of your process. What are the big steps that will take your client from point A to point B? 3–5 maximum. In your work, is it a "before-during-after?" or a "diet-exercise-lifestyle?"

Find your big 3 to 5 max because no one trusts 11 steps. Here's a fun reason to stop at five steps: it's the most steps you can show with one hand while you speak!

2. Steps Within Each Phase

These are the "things" within each phase or pillar that achieve that particular goal of the phase or pillar. Again: 3–5 maximum. Think of them like bullet points. If your topic is sales, maybe your 3 phases are a version of the "before-during-after" model for a sales meeting. What would be your 3 steps in your "before" (the meeting) phase? Maybe it would be "qualifying the prospect - agreement of meeting - pre-indoctrination materials."

That's it. Your micro-steps are suppressed. HINT: Your micro-steps are fuel for content. More on that in Part Three.

3. Visual Simplicity (Grid / Graph / Map)

This is the part most experts skip. When you make it visual, you make it real. Can you show a 3x3 matrix? Perhaps a ladder or a simple arc. When you do, you are signaling "This has structure." Structure shows the world that you have a plan. And people want to work with experts who have a plan.

4. Naming the Phases

I repeat *"name your shit"* because it is that important. If you don't name the phases, you don't own the path, and you will blend in with the mediocre majority that repeat the generic terms they learned in training. Names create memory and allow repetition, and repetition creates brand. That's why your framework is so valuable to you.

5. Clarifying Process Gates

At the end of each phase, there should be a question like: *"Are you ready to move from awareness to action?"* *"Have you clarified your position before promoting?"* These clarifications show your client's progress.

I — INTEGRATE YOUR DOCTRINE EVERYWHERE

This is the fun part. You have documented and created your own language and lingo; now you can shout it from the rooftops!

Integration Creates Recognition

When your doctrine appears consistently, people begin to recognize your thinking and begin to associate it with your name. Anyone can post content, but very few people have **recognizable patterns of thought**, and recognition of thinking is what builds authority. When your ideas appear repeatedly across posts, emails, talks, and conversations, people start to recognize you, and that is the beginning of brand authority.

Intentional Repetition Is Not Redundancy

Most people are afraid of repeating themselves. Experts repeat themselves constantly. Why?

Ideas need **multiple exposures** before they become associated with you. The same idea can appear as:

- a short post
- a longer article
- a story

- an example with a case study
- a diagram you explain
- a question you answer

Different format, but the same doctrine. Repetition is how ideas become **owned**. Think about how a musician scores a hit record. After multiple exposures, you suddenly find yourself singing along and know all the words without trying. That's the kind of recognition you want.

Doctrine Simplifies Content Creation

Once your matrix exists, you no longer ask *"What should I post today?"* Instead, you ask, *"How does today's content express my doctrine?"* Your framework becomes the filter. Content stops feeling random and starts feeling like **documentation.**

Integration Compounds Authority

When every piece of content reflects the same doctrine, something powerful happens. You go from simply being recognized to being seen as the "go-to-expert" on your subject. People see the same ideas across:

- your posts
- your emails
- your videos
- your talks
- your book
- your conversations

The repetition signals expertise and earned wisdom, which creates trust.

Integration Makes Your Thinking Transferable

Your doctrine is now your unmistakable intellectual property. When your doctrine appears everywhere, it becomes teachable. When *others* begin talking about your concepts, they are glorifying YOU. Then, you become a legend!

Did you know that the ideas living only inside your head were this valuable?

Integration Gives You a Web

Once you get integration down, random content disappears, and content assets accumulate. Every piece becomes another doorway into your thinking. A prospect might discover you through an article, a podcast clip, a social post, an email, or maybe a video. But they all lead to the same system. If all of these different media channels were like a spider web, no matter where they discover you, you've got them in your web, so you can capture their heartshare.

As your doctrine appears across your posts, emails, talks, and conversations, something important begins to happen. People begin to see a **pattern of thinking**. The ideas start to feel connected, and your language becomes recognizable. Your framework becomes easier to explain and easier to remember. At that point, your doctrine is no longer only something you use; it is something people **associate with you**. And once that happens, the final step becomes obvious.

You've framed it. You've named it. You've made it unmistakably yours. Now, your next step is to claim it! That is where real authority begins.

C — CLAIM YOUR FAME

For the first time, I'm granting you permission to name what you do and make it famous. Maybe you resisted it because you felt it seemed arrogant to do that. I don't think it's arrogant, I think it's responsible. If you know that what you do can help a lot of people, then you have a responsibility to do whatever it takes for people to easily understand the help you have to offer.

Maybe you felt like naming your things would make you seem like a guru, and that's the last thing you want to be seen as. You're not claiming to know everything; you're claiming the way that you do things. When you name your method, you make your thinking easier for people to understand, discuss, and share.

Authority Is Claimed, Not Granted

No one appoints you as the authority in your field. You declare it. But you don't do it by shouting. You do it by sharing your wisdom through your matrix. The experts people remember are the ones who were willing to say, *"This is how I see it." "This is how it works."* If you hesitate to claim your thinking, you'll kick yourself each time you see someone else's version.

Ownership Signals Confidence

People trust people who appear certain about how they work. When you clearly state your approach and your framework and say, *"This is how I help people solve this problem,"* you signal conviction. And that conviction will attract the right people and repel the wrong ones.

Your Signature Authority Book
Becomes the Flag in the Ground

A book is the strongest way to claim your intellectual territory. It memorializes your thinking in one place. It gives your framework structure. And your ideas trigger meaningful conversations and initial meetings, and remain memorable long after a conversation ends.

Within Part Three, in one of the chapters, you'll discover the life-changing magic of a Signature Authority Book and how it will become the foundation of your business. Your book becomes the place people point to when they say, *"This is the person who teaches that."*

I hope you have discovered that your thinking was never the problem. The problem was that it lived only in conversations, scattered explanations, and moments of insight that disappeared after they were spoken. When you memorialize your magic, integrate it everywhere, and boldly claim it as your own, something powerful happens...

The work you have done for years finally becomes what it always deserved to be: What you are known for.

In the next part, we move from defining your doctrine to deploying it through cashflow content that transforms your ideas into authority and revenue-driving assets.

KEY TAKEAWAYS

- Capture, organize, and memorialize your best ideas, so they compound and last beyond a single conversation.

- Clarify your mission so the right people instantly recognize themselves and know why to care now.

- Articulate your process to turn invisible instinct into visible doctrine and transform experience into authority.

- When you guide people with a clear structure, simple phases, and memorable language, your expertise becomes easier to understand, trust, and follow.

- Your authority grows when your doctrine appears everywhere, and you confidently claim the ideas, frameworks, and language that unmistakably mark your thinking as yours.

PART THREE

THE CASHFLOW CONTENT METHOD

TURNING DOCTRINE INTO AUTHORITY, DEMAND, AND REVENUE

. . . .

"What you can explain once might impress.
What you can express repeatedly will pay you."

—MARK IMPERIAL

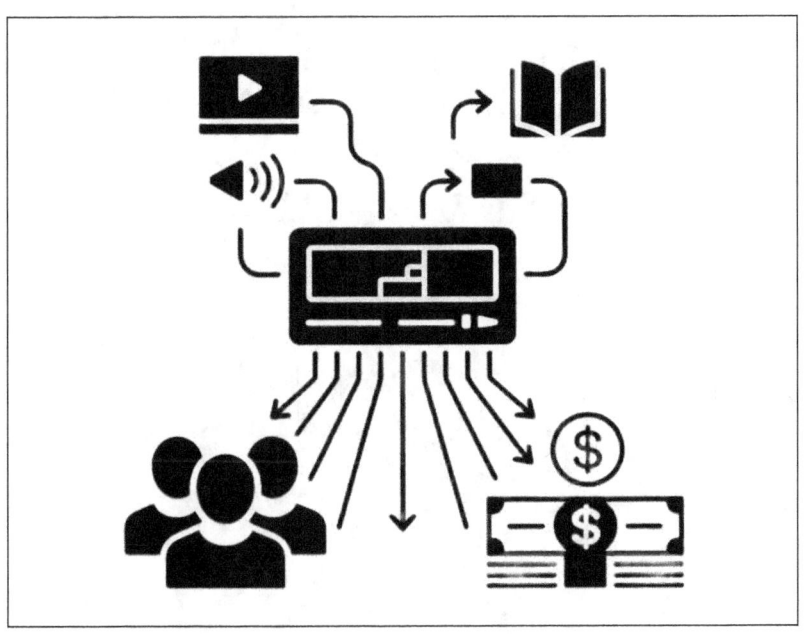

THE KNOWN-FOR EFFECT

How People Choose You for What You're Known-For, and Trust, Demand, and Revenue Compound

....

"The great enemy of communication is the illusion of it."

—WILLIAM H. WHYTE

....

As we discussed in Part Two, ideas shared only behind closed doors vanish after the meeting. If they're not shared, no one will ever associate you with them. Part Two showed you how to uncover and record your strengths. In Part Three, you'll learn how to share them publicly.

Many experts believe their reputation reflects their expertise. But in reality, the marketplace can only recognize ideas it **repeatedly encounters.** That's why some professionals with enormous knowledge remain largely invisible, while others become known for something very specific. Their ideas **circulate.**

This creates a gap between what someone knows and what people know them for. As a reminder, I call that the **Known-For Gap.**

When that gap closes, and what you know and what people associate you with finally align, the **Known-For Effect** takes hold: the point where your ideas circulate, your name attaches to them, and your authority, trust, demand, and revenue begin to compound without additional effort.

In this chapter, you'll discover what occurs when your ideas stop vanishing in conversations and begin circulating in the marketplace—where recognition accelerates, trust strengthens, and people select you before you even speak to them.

AUTHORITY COMES FROM DOCUMENTED THINKING

A few years ago, I was helping a client plan her forthcoming book. She's an Exit Planning Advisor (CEPA) who helps business owners maximize the value of their businesses when they're ready to sell. She had been in the industry for more than twenty years.

As we talked, she casually explained how she handled a common problem that many of her clients struggled with. Her explanation was clear, insightful, and incredibly helpful.

When she finished, I asked her a simple question. *"Where have you written that down?"*

She looked at me and said, *"I haven't."* Furthermore, she said, *"It's nothing unique, I just use the same process all CEPAs are certified for, I just do a few things differently, and I do them in a slightly different order."*

Her insights had lived entirely in conversations for years, and she had probably explained them hundreds of times to clients. Two missed opportunities there: 1) Outside those conversations, the marketplace had never seen her ideas or her...and...2) Because she does things a *"little differently and in a slightly different order,"* that makes her way proprietary, and she didn't **frame it, name it, or claim it!** (Remember "the notes were already there before Beethoven came along?") She wrote an <u>entirely new song</u>, which meant her ideas were disappearing like the spark from a firework as it fell to the ground. And if an idea disappears after it's shared, the market never gets the chance to recognize you for it. Out of sight, out of mind.

When you capture and document your ideas elegantly, they become discoverable, memorable, and attributed to you. Record your ideas today; sharing them forever will give you ultimate leverage and scalability! Now you don't have to worry about "creating novel content," you can merely focus on turning your existing thinking into content.

LIFE IS A MOVING PARADE

Ideas are like floats in a parade. Each one is elegant in its own way. When you see one, you're eager to see the next, and the next, and the next. It doesn't "really" matter which order you see the floats; As long as they aren't boring, you keep watching. Parades bring joy. They make an impression. You remember them, and you tell others what you saw.

THIS is your content. Your content should grab attention, wow them by showing they've discovered something so valuable they can't help but tell others about it, give them confidence that you are the person they want to work with, and keep them wanting more. They may have discovered you from your first piece of content, or your 200th. It doesn't matter as long as you hook them into wanting more. That is why, against what you may have heard about cadence or consistency, it doesn't matter what the cadence is. When you do this right, your content will be evergreen, and your footprint will compound. Once people discover an expert from a piece of content that hooked them, what do you think they do next?

They think, *"Who is this?" "Why haven't I heard of them before?" "What else can I hear from them?"* **"Do they have a book?"** See that? People know they can quickly figure out who someone is and what they stand for simply by looking at their book. Notice I didn't even say "read their book." A proper title, subtitle, and back cover copy will tell them enough to know whether the author is for them. More on the life-changing power of a book in Chapter Ten.

Experts gain authority through repeated encounters with ideas. You don't need much. Just your magic finally distilled as we did in Part Two. That set of ideas can be repurposed in different media. They should be memorialized in a book. They could be made into a podcast. They can be a YouTube video series. Intentional redundancy without appearing redundant. Just like your favorite artist performing your favorite song in different contexts: the original studio version, live in concert, acoustic "unplugged" version, a cappella, remix, lounge version. It's the same tune, and you're enjoying it in different ways. With your content, you find different ways to illustrate the same key pillars of knowledge. The more intentional redundancy, the more "known-for" you will become.

HOW RECOGNITION FORMS

People think you have to be a never-ending river of knowledge and come up with new discoveries all the time. The reality is that the most famous experts who have ever lived are known for the mastery of a single concept, not exhaustive knowledge!

Dave Ramsey has a boatload of financial knowledge, but he became famous not for spouting something new every week, but from beating his "Financial Peace" drum and letting you know his enemy is debt, while finding different ways to illustrate those same two points. Albert Einstein could have given a clinic with his broad work in Physics, but his fame rests solely on his formula $E=mc^2$ and relativity.

CONTENT ALLOWS YOU TO
TRANSCEND TIME

Circulating your ideas allows people to discover you now, months from now, years from now, and even allows those ideas to live beyond you. You are creating a body of work that grows and compounds. It expands your footprint, digital and in real life. Conditions align for different people at different times. When someone searches for help in your zone of genius, ideally, *your* magic appears.

How about leaving a legacy? Early ideas seed later breakthroughs. This book is the result of many, many things I've learned from many, many different people and places. I merely curated them and injected the most priceless element: **my judgment.** One day, even when you're gone, someone may quote your work as the inspiration for their innovation.

Life is a moving parade of ideas, where each float, your distilled magic, your planet's own catchy language, like "time vampires," or timeless SOPs, captivates on its own vivid merit. Forget obsessing over rigid posting schedules or cadence; audiences stay mesmerized by the parade's momentum, eagerly chasing standout pieces that spark discovery and curiosity. Drop your evergreen content when it shines brightest, let intentional redundancy across books, videos, and podcasts propel it forward, and watch your authority compound as viewers seek you out organically now, months later, or years down the line.

EVERYTHING NEW IS ACTUALLY OLD

One day, I heard someone say, *"Newsletter marketing is the NEW thing!"* I thought, *"What the hell?! I had a newsletter for my DJs Edge Marketing members in 2008. I wrote for Dan Kennedy's No BS Marketing Letter for 3 years. How can this be NEW?"*

Being the marketing nerd I am, having started way back in the 1900s, I had to hear more, so I listened to some podcasts about this growing trend of "newsletter marketing." It didn't take more than 2 minutes for my suspicions to be validated. **This is nothing more than email marketing!** The e-zine queen, Alexandria Brown, was the first to coin this as an "e-zine" back in the early 2000s. It's nothing more than a fancy way to say *"Bribe them to give you their email address, then spam the hell out of them until they buy, die, or unsubscribe!"* I say "spam" in fun; I really mean *"Give them tons of value until they want to do business with you or tell you to F*** off."*

All that gyration to tell you that everything you see was invented 100+ years ago, done with rocks and crayons before the internet came along. And the point of making this point is to point out (that's a lot of points) that you can instantly demystify whatever the hell people want you to believe "content marketing" is by seeing it for the only thing it is: **FOLLOW UP.**

Way back in the 90s, when I was a DJ, we would exhibit at bridal expos. I would get everyone's mailing address and phone number. My shorts are tightening just thinking about it. After the expo, we would call each bride to set up a face-to-face meeting. (I just heard a *gasp* from every millennial and younger reading this.) Yes, we had to talk on the phone and meet people face to face.

Before the meeting, I would mail them a VHS highlight reel, my book "The Ultimate Wedding Reception," and photocopies of 2 dozen endorsement letters from past clients.

I'm dating myself, however, I think it's useful to illustrate that the internet did nothing more than give us a cheaper and faster way to achieve a lot of the same, however, not without its pitfalls. Modern content simply mimics exactly everything we did before the internet, just easier. We grew our "mailing list" not with email addresses but with street addresses to mail stuff.

On at least a monthly basis, to stay top of mind with our market of buyers and non-buyers, we would mail a print newsletter (and you still should today). With the internet, we can now increase the frequency so you can do weekly, if not daily, "newsletter" emails. These physical newsletters contained amusing stories, client mentions, and answer-based marketing. Answer-based marketing is the answer to the market's most frequently asked questions. Market education. We would interact with our tribe, and they would write in (I even had an 800 number where they could call and leave their questions on a toll-free voicemail system). This was the original social media!

The moral is, if you simply view your "content" the way we communicated with pen, paper, and stamps, you won't be so overwhelmed by the thought of it. Content is nothing more than good communication between a business and its community.

WHY SOME IDEAS STICK

The experts who become "known-for" are the ones who made their ideas memorable. They did this a few different ways. As we discussed in Part Two, they finally started documenting their standard operating procedures (SOPs). They stripped out the minute details and created simplified phases and steps so anyone can easily follow. They gave their processes catchy names that opened people's eyes. They described their prospects' problems better than they could, and they gave their enemies novel names like "time vampires!"

Ideas stick best when people feel like they **discovered them themselves.** When people feel like they're being told something, it's often forgettable. But when they arrive at the insight on their own, the idea feels personal, and personal ideas tend to stick. For example, instead of simply telling someone, *"People who steal your time are time vampires,"* you could ask a question:

"What would you call someone who constantly sucks up your time and energy until you feel drained?"

Most people pause for a moment. Then the image appears. A vampire. Now, when you say, *"call them time vampires,"* the idea lands differently. It doesn't feel like something you just told them. It feels like something they realized.

Another consideration is that information and facts merely *tell*, while stories *sell*. Another huge point of documentation is to catalog your stories! Go through your matrix and see how many stories you can recall that illustrate each phase or step. Catalog them! A story about what inspired you to do what you do is called an **origin story.** Catalog your origin story or stories because when you subtly pepper them into your content, it signals to your market that you're doing it from your heart, not just for the money (and hopefully you are).

When an idea becomes visual, memorable, and easy to name, it becomes easier for people to remember and repeat. In 1948, McDonald's called their revolutionary assembly-line production **The Speedee Service System.** This system focused on speed, efficiency, and a limited menu to deliver burgers, fries, and drinks in about 30 seconds. You'll probably remember that, and I didn't even go into the lengthy tour of how it works. **"Got Milk?"** boosted milk consumption 7% by making milk cool without explaining why. The marketplace rarely remembers explanations; it remembers what things are called.

Naming ideas and creating brands helps you become "known-for" something by creating proprietary concepts that the market associates exclusively with you, building authority and recall in a crowded field. Your brand is the anchor in your market's mind.

Closing the **Known-For Gap,** the divide between what you know and what people associate you with, shows progress when your unique ideas gain traction and public linkage. Signs that your ideas are starting to circulate are when people start referencing your concepts, like when I hear students casually mention my concepts and say, *"Use the M.A.G.I.C framework"* in industry chats. Or, crediting my ActionBrand™ approach in posts. Or I'll get a referral, and they say, *"I heard you're the ActionBrand™ guy."* Or *"You're the Known-for guy!"* If someone attributes my tagline, *"Turn what you know into what you're known for,"* it's a content echo, telling me people are taking notice. Do you see what's happening here? It's a little meta, I know, that this entire book is an illustration of all the principles in action. Well, you can't say I don't practice what I preach.

It's important to be intentional in how you present things because it is in the comfort of the repetition that things get anchored in the mind. Hearing something once is forgettable; a second time, perhaps a coincidence; but 7 to 20 times, now there's real cognitive anchoring going on, and people will begin to finish your sentences.

OWNING YOUR PLATFORM. BORROWING AUTHORITY AND REACH

Multiple media reinforce the anchor. Posts deliver the core idea. Talks and podcasts add voice and personality, and video puts a face to the name, bringing your concepts to life. Short-form content suits skimmers, but more importantly, it draws them to your long-form, where conversion really happens. My mentor always said, *"They won't give you money if they're unwilling to give you their time first."* Podcasts are another way to engage people in your long-form content with stories. Then, books are the ultimate apex asset of long-form content that attract committed learners. And committed learners become your best clients.

This entire book is about establishing and distributing your own intellectual property (IP). Expressing your IP on your own platforms is where we are going. But I don't want you to stop there. Your authority and reach will accelerate when you start to show up on other people's platforms. Appearing on other established or rising business owner creators' platforms lets you borrow their reach. Swap appearances. You interview them for your show, and vice versa. If they're a known authority and you interview them for your platform, it signals that you play with the big dogs in the tall grass. And just like Nintendo™, you're playing with power.

THE LADDER OF AUTHORITY PLATFORMS

Before we explore "what" your content should consist of, we need to briefly touch on the type of media platforms to use. There is a hierarchy of value among platforms. You don't have to do all of them; however, the more the merrier.

Let's start at the bottom. All businesses should, at a minimum, communicate with their markets, customers, clients, and prospects through a regular mechanism. This should be at least once per week. You can use an email "newsletter." A print on one would be better.

A step up is a blog. While not as popular today, it's a place connected to your website where you post. The idea is that when you notify your list by email of your latest post, it brings them back to your blog. Blogs are okay; however, they're not organized to deliver your message as orderly as in a book.

CASHFLOW CONTENT

—— VALUE LADDER

AUTHOR
THE APEX ASSET

SPEAKING

YOUTUBE

PODCAST

BLOGS

NEWSLETTER

Next up the ladder would be some type of show. This can be a podcast or YouTube channel. If you're comfortable on camera or a microphone, a show is a powerful tool. Collaboration with other show hosts is one of the most effective ways to get your voice out there. Swap appearances on each other's shows. By the way, a powerful way to be invited as a guest on other shows is to have a book because authors are highly desirable to show hosts. And podcast guesting is in the top 2 ways to promote a book and get known. I always say, *"Give 'em something to talk about! (your book.)"*

Next up is speaking. Speaking is the number one way to gain authority and spread your message. It's also the number one way to promote a book. And published authors are the most attractive to event promoters for their stages. A book-and-speaking combo is your ultimate 1-2 punch.

That leads us to the Apex Asset, which is a book. If you've noticed on the ladder, authorship 10x's the power of all the other platforms. And if you don't desire the spotlight at all, your book will do all the work for you, so it's a no-brainer. That's how utility books are. They're client-getting, authority assets. And you'll discover what you need to know about them in Chapter Ten.

You're creating an amazing web of authority and validation. Demonstrations of confidence and capability, signals of wisdom, all cross-reference each other. *"As I shared in my podcast..." "In my book..."* is all self-perpetuating validation of expertise.

When you hear your branded concepts being echoed by peers and strangers in unrelated conversations, and people begin referring to you by your "known-for" moniker at least weekly, then you know you're closing the **Known-For Gap.**

If someone reading this book had extraordinary expertise but was almost invisible in their industry, I would tell them to start simplifying how they explain their concepts. Humans favor simple concepts and run away from complex ones. I describe it this way: humans are always looking for shortcuts. The simplest way to describe something. The simplest way to understand something. The easy button. The easier you make it for people to understand you, the more you will become "known-for" your thing.

Before we fire up the content engine, we need to understand something first: how ideas spread. Because ideas don't spread randomly. They spread according to how humans decide what matters.

KEY TAKEAWAYS

- Authority begins the moment your thinking stops disappearing inside conversations and starts living somewhere the market can repeatedly encounter it.

- The market cannot recognize what it cannot see, so closing the **Known-For Gap** means turning the ideas you explain every day into documented, discoverable content.

- You do not need endless new insights. You need a few clear ideas expressed memorably, repeated intentionally, and experienced across multiple forms of media.

- Ideas stick when they are simple, named, visual, and easy to repeat. The easier you make it for people to remember your concepts, the easier it becomes for them to associate those concepts with you.

- When people begin referencing your frameworks, repeating your language, and introducing you by what you are known for, your ideas are circulating, and your authority is compounding.

WHY IDEAS SPREAD AND DECISIONS ARE MADE

The Hidden Forces That Drive Every Choice

. . . .

"Human beings are moved less by what is and more by what they imagine could be."

—MARK IMPERIAL

. . . .

Before we discuss the specific types of content you should create, let's talk about what actually motivates humans into action. Many people assume decisions are logical and rational. They think it's as simple as gathering information, weighing the facts, and choosing the best option. If that were true, marketing formulas wouldn't have survived for over a century, speeches wouldn't move crowds, and ideas wouldn't spread the way they do.

Most decisions are not driven solely by logic. When I was a young marketing student, I was taught that people make decisions emotionally and justify them with logic afterward. Over time, I've come to believe something even more powerful. Human beings are moved less by what *is* and more by what they imagine *could* be.

You've seen this play out before. Think about a character in a TV show who stays in a relationship that isn't healthy. From the outside, it's obvious they're not in love with who the person actually is, but with who they hope they could become. People fall in love with possibility, not reality. And that same dynamic shows up in how decisions are made.

This tendency also explains why people act only when something becomes personally important. Remember the last time something captured your attention in a meaningful way? Maybe it was a business idea, a book, or a problem you suddenly realized you had to solve. That idea may have lingered unnoticed until a shift in your priorities made it relevant.

Life is constantly moving. Like a parade, different floats come into view at different times, and what captures your attention depends on where you're standing at that moment. The same is true with ideas, opportunities, and problems. What matters to someone today may not have mattered last year, and it may not matter to someone else for years to come. That's why you have to stay visible. You can't predict the exact moment when someone's priorities will align with what you have to say. The best strategy is to make sure your ideas are always in motion, so when that moment comes, you're there.

When beliefs and priorities finally line up with your message, what once felt invisible suddenly becomes important. When it becomes a priority, people begin to notice it everywhere; they look for it and act on it. In marketing, we describe prospects in this state as "in heat"; their priority is active now.

Underneath every decision are two forces: **awareness** and **persuasion**. Awareness drives what people notice; without it, ideas stay invisible. Persuasion shapes what matters once an idea is seen. Does it solve a problem, enable progress, or offer protection?

Decisions occur when awareness and persuasion intersect. This explains why some ideas spread easily while others don't. The ones that connect with what people already care about, even if people hadn't articulated it before, are the ones that grow. Once people see themselves reflected in an idea, they begin to share, repeat, and explain it to others.

Awareness determines when someone can hear you. Persuasion determines whether they act.

READ THE ROOM: WHY AWARENESS CHANGES EVERYTHING

Eugene Schwartz explained that people move through different levels of awareness before making a decision. Some don't know they have a problem yet. Others know the problem but not the solution. Some know the solution, but not the product or plan that can help them. Others are already familiar with a plan but not a provider. And the most aware are ready to act when they have all the information about the providers and how to compare them, so they can make an informed decision about whom to hire.

Most communication fails because it ignores this. Often, people present solutions to those who don't see the problem or make offers before the audience is ready, so the message falls flat. The right idea at the wrong moment is invisible. But when someone's awareness shifts, something they've seen before suddenly stands out. A message they ignored now feels obvious. Nothing about the message changed. The person did.

When you understand this, marketing stops feeling like manipulation and starts looking more like interpretation. The most effective communicators help people see something in a way that suddenly makes sense, and that is when decisions are made.

WHY PERSUASION
FORMULAS STILL WORK

Marketing books are filled with formulas like AIDA, Problem-Agitate-Solve, and Picture-Promise-Proof-Proposal. These formulas have survived for more than a century for a simple reason. People still want relief, reassurance, proof, belonging, hope, and a reason to take action. That's what these formulas are organizing. They're not magic. They're patterns that reflect how people make decisions.

That's also why there is more than one way to be right. Different formulas can all work because they draw from the same underlying motivations. People will try to convince you that marketing online is different, but it's not. It's simply another medium. What worked in print still works online because people haven't changed. I still miss the days of paper, ink, envelopes, and stamps. There was something about receiving a sales letter that felt different. Did you know that direct mail still outperforms most digital channels in response rates? People should really check their math and see if it *really* made sense to abandon it!

WHAT HUMANS PRIORITIZE

At the core of every decision is a simple question, even if people never say it out loud. *Does this matter to me right now?* When you step back and look at persuasion frameworks, you start to notice they're all doing the same thing. They may use different words or structures, but underneath, they're organizing communication around what humans already value.

#1 Survival and Security: The foundation of literally every decision

#2 Health and Vitality: Relief from pain and seeking well-being and longevity

#3 Money and Wealth: Make more by doing less is a top hook

#4 Love and Belonging: Companionship, family, and social approval

#5 Status and Achievement: Pride, prestige, praise, and superiority

#6 Comfort and Convenience: Save time & effort and a desire for ease

#7 Self-Improvement: Desire for confidence & capabilities

#8 Enjoyment and Pleasure: Fun experiences and adventure seeking

Notice how some drivers stack. For example, money raises status and drives survival, security, and companionship, and also pays for fun adventures. Every formula is a different way of guiding someone from where they are to a decision that feels right to them. That's why they all work, but that's also why business owners get overwhelmed. They think they need to master every formula, every structure, every variation. They don't. Some marketers live their entire career using one formula. Besides, for most of your content, you won't be creating long-form infomercials.

The real skill is understanding what people care about and learning how to speak to those priorities clearly. In Maslow's hierarchy of needs, the lower levels must be satisfied before higher-level desires take over. The same principle applies here.

MASLOW'S HIERARCHY OF NEEDS

SELF-ACTUALIZATION
desire to become the most
that one can be

ESTEEM
respect, self-esteem, status,
recognition, strength, freedom

LOVE AND BELONGING:
friendship, intimacy, family,
sense of connection

SAFETY NEEDS:
personal security, employment,
resources, health, property

PHYSIOLOGICAL NEEDS:
air, water, food, shelter, sleep,
clothing, reproduction

INFLUENCE, SIMPLIFIED

Copywriter Blair Warren captured the essence of influence in a single sentence: *"People will do anything for those who encourage their dreams, justify their failures, allay their fears, confirm their suspicions, and help them throw rocks at their enemies."* That sentence reveals five powerful psychological drivers behind human behavior. And here's the good news. You don't have to hit all five. If a single piece of content connects with even one of these drivers, it can resonate with a segment of your audience. Use this as a filter. One driver, one message, one piece of content. It's the best way to stop blending in and start becoming known for something!

DROWNING IN A SEA OF CONTENT

I recently spoke with a business owner who felt invisible. He told me he already felt behind because he hadn't been creating content, and now with AI, he believed his message would get lost in all the noise. You've probably heard some version of this, or maybe you've thought it yourself. And in one sense, it's true. There has never been more content being published. But that's not the real problem.

The real problem is that most content sounds the same. This happens when new platforms emerge: voices stand out at first, then best practices and templates spread, making content feel predictable and forgettable.

Content doesn't stop working. It turns into a commodity. And that's where the advantage shifts in your favor. It no longer belongs to the person who produces the most. It belongs to the person who stands out the most. When content turns into a commodity, mindshare shifts to the messenger. And when information is interchangeable, personality is paramount.

People stop looking for more information and start looking for someone who can make sense of it. **The Interpreter.** Someone whose way of explaining things just clicks. Someone who can translate complexity into clarity. **The Navigator.** That's why I declare the next age to be the **Navigator Economy.** In a world where everyone can publish, sounding like everyone else is the fastest way to disappear. From this point forward, everything you publish is intentional. When your thinking is clear, and your voice is unmistakable, your ideas don't get lost. They shine!

PEOPLE FOLLOW PEOPLE, NOT JUST IDEAS

If this still feels overwhelming, boil it down to two things: Where someone is and what they care about. Awareness tells you where they are. Human motivation tells you what matters to them. Every framework you've ever seen is a way of organizing those two things. You don't need to master everything or chase trends. Just say things that connect.

In a world where content is a commodity, that connection comes from sounding like you. People follow people. And when your thinking is clear and visible, **what you know becomes what you're known for.**

KEY TAKEAWAYS

- People act because something is meaningful to them in that moment, and beliefs and priorities finally line up.

- Awareness and persuasion drive every decision. If someone cannot see it or cannot connect it to what they value, nothing happens.

- Every formula works because it taps into the same human priorities. You do not need to master them all; you need to understand what matters to people right now.

- The real problem is too much sameness. When content turns into a commodity, mindshare shifts to the messenger.

- You win by meeting people where they are, speaking to what they care about, and showing up with a voice that is unmistakably yours.

THE CASHFLOW CONTENT ENGINE

A System That Produces Attention, Trust, and Action

....

*"Content doesn't catch fire by chance.
It happens by design."*

—MARK IMPERIAL

....

At this point, you already understand something most people never figure out. Neither content, visibility, nor consistency is the problem. The real problem is that most content doesn't carry forward. It gets posted, and then it disappears. Which means no matter how much you create, you're constantly starting over. Like hitting a reset button.

So let's fast-forward to the part you've been waiting for. Everything you've discovered becomes something that actually works!

THE CASHFLOW CONTENT ENGINE

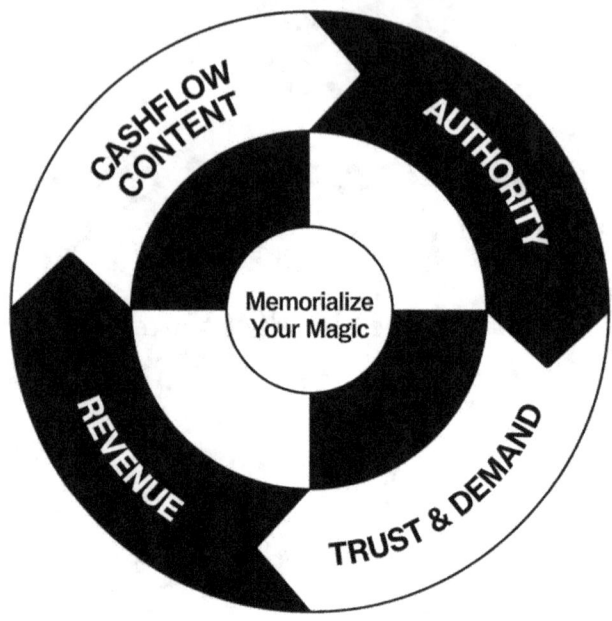

Authority compounds when
expertise becomes visible.

WHAT SHOULD I POST... AND WHERE?

By now, you might be thinking, *"Okay, Mark... just tell me what to post and where to post it."* Fair enough! What I'm going to give you is even better than that. It just might not be what you expect. This book is evergreen because the principles don't change regardless of the platform you deploy it on. Platforms and features come and go. Algorithms change. Get over it. What doesn't change are the fundamentals of marketing.

So with that in mind, instead of chasing channels, we're going to build something far more valuable: assets that work no matter the platform. If you build this the right way and the algorithm disappears tomorrow, your assets won't.

Assets Over Algorithms

Most people study media, but few study marketing. They don't know what they don't know, so they grab the next shiny platform training: TikTok, Facebook, Insta, X, or whatever's next. They learn how to post on the platform, but not what to post, so they share crap that doesn't work, and worse, makes them look bad!

You don't need to master every platform. You need to master the message because it's what travels and sells. Let the "new media" experts worry about the algorithms. Your job is to create content that matters, carries, and compounds.

Stay in Your Lane

If you're a business owner, be a business owner. If you're an expert, be the expert. Don't turn yourself into a part-time platform technician. Remember, if the content itself isn't strong, no platform will save it. Instead, focus on what actually moves the needle: clear thinking, messaging, and communication, because that's the leverage and what you do every day in your work.

A NOTE ON WHERE TO START

Now, with that said, you do have to start somewhere. So here's a rule: Pick one channel and go all in. Not forever, just long enough to build momentum. Once you have built a foundation on that channel, you can repurpose it for another channel.

If you're a strong writer, start with written content. If you're better on video, lean into video. Play to your strengths because if you're not comfortable, it will be too easy for you to quit.

And here's a helpful way to think about platforms when choosing: Some platforms are **feeds**. Others are **libraries**.

Feeds move fast. Content appears and disappears. Feeds have their purpose, but they're not for foundations.

Libraries store value. Content lives and can be accessed at random. It gets discovered, and it keeps working long after you create it. That's why long-form content, especially video, can be so powerful. YouTube stores your knowledge in an easy-to-access, easy-to-navigate format.

But again, this isn't about the platform; it's about the principle. No matter where you publish, the goal remains the same: create something that lasts.

FROM POSTING TO BUILDING

I remember working with a business owner who thought they were doing everything "right," posting consistently, showing up weekly, and sometimes even putting in daily effort into their content.

I asked them a simple question: *"What are you known for?"*

They paused. Not because they weren't good at what they did, but because nothing they were posting was sticking. Every post lived and died on its own. They were posting on a feed (Facebook, to be exact). They said that's what they were taught to do, but nothing got traction.

Why? The reality was they were on a hamster wheel. None of their content compounded. They'd post in the morning; less than 1% saw it. Nothing happened. They'd post in the afternoon; a different half-percent saw it, but not the prior post. They would run out of ideas to post, so it became random. They weren't building content. They were resetting the clock every time they posted.

They're not alone. Most people think they're creating content, but really they're slinging crap and hoping something "catches." Instead, they get a few likes and one comment, then poof! It's gone. Nothing builds, nothing compounds, no memory in the marketplace. For readers, the parade moves on.

When content is built to compound, your ideas gain momentum and continue working for you, long after you hit publish. An engine generates power. A flywheel makes that power smooth and sustainable. Your content is what spins the flywheel. At first, it takes effort, but once it's moving, it gets easier, faster, and it starts working for you.

That's the Cashflow Content Engine. Your thinking generates the spin. The engine multiplies your exposure, recognition, authority, and opportunity. And your content keeps it running.

CONTENT HAS JOBS

I've also seen the opposite problem. I've seen someone who creates incredible educational content, but they remain completely invisible.

Why?

Because all they ever did was teach. They ignored creating attraction and didn't talk about the problem they were solving. It was like giving a masterclass in an empty room. The content was good, but it wasn't doing its job.

Very few understand what their content is supposed to do. Every piece of content must have a job: Attract attention, build trust, demonstrate expertise, create engagement, invite action, or expand reach. Each post moves someone forward or leaves them where they are. Content without a purpose is just noise.

For me, this clicked in a very specific moment. I was looking at everything I had created over the years that always worked predictably: talks, posts, books, and conversations, and I noticed that I wasn't following a calendar. I was naturally cycling through a handful of content types repeatedly. I was attracting attention, expanding on ideas, teaching what I knew, engaging people, inviting action, and connecting with others. It wasn't random. It was a rotating system. A flywheel. I just hadn't named it yet. <u>And bold this because it is the key:</u> **Everything you're about to discover, I built it all for my physical mailing list and email list first, and you should, too.** Before I ever put any of it on the socials, it was already quietly making 100% of my revenue just from my lists for years! I want you to fully hear that because it is that important.

Social platforms just became another media you can use to repurpose what already works.

At some point, I realized that great content only needs to accomplish a few key things. Once you know what those are, you stop guessing and overcomplicating what to create.

BEFORE WE TURN ON THE ENGINE

Before I show you how to create content consistently, I want to show you something that will make everything easier. You'll build your **foundation first.** Most people think content starts with posting, but it really starts with clarity, which begins by laying a foundation. As I mentioned, build your email list foundation first *(and your physical mail, if you have that, too).* If you want, you can host your videos on a platform like YouTube, as long as you use your email list to send them to watch. Double-whammy. Your foundation is an asset you create once, and it works for you forever. In this case, your foundation is your perfect end-to-end pitch that turns prospects into clients. Keep reading.

One of the most valuable things I learned early on is this: **Before you build the product, write the sales letter.** When it's still "fantasy," you give yourself permission to think bigger. You design the ideal outcome rather than take what exists and try to find where to sell it. You get to design the user's dream outcome. Then later, you trim it back to reality, to what is physically and economically possible. But now you know what you're building toward. That single exercise gives you something most people never get: Direction.

And here's the best part...

That sales letter? Done right, it is the foundation for everything.

Step One: Write the Message

Write the sales letter, or you can look at it as a stage presentation, or a long-form video script, whatever floats your boat.

In this message, you're answering:

- *What problem do you solve?*
- *Why does it matter?*
- *What's a better way?*
- *Why should someone trust you?*

This gives you a clear end-to-end picture.

Step Two: Turn It Into a Long-Form Asset

Now turn that into one piece of long-form content. A 30 to 60-minute video, presentation, or webinar. The only 2 "must-haves" are clarity and personality. This becomes your **core asset.**

Step Three: Multiply It

Take that long-form piece and break it into smaller chunks. Have an editor chop it up for future highlights, clips, shorts, reels. Now you don't just have "content ideas," you have **content supply.** And that supply is thorough and complete.

Step Four: "Put 'Em in the Box"

A colleague of mine used to say something that stuck with me: *"Put 'em in the box."* What he meant was that every piece of content should lead the recipient to one place, one doorway into your world. A landing page with an opt-in "box." This is your email collection device.

To connect, you have to collect! Collect a contact list. Your email list will become the most valuable thing your business owns. More valuable than your inventory and tools, because none of that matters unless you know who you can sell them to. So every piece of content ends with some version of: *"If you found this helpful, go here and let's connect."* (implying "get more" or "get the rest.")

Step Five: Build Your Follow-Up Engine

Now it gets powerful. Your content isn't random anymore; it's a **nurture sequence.** For example, if you met someone at a conference… what would you send them next? That's your content. Think about it like this: 80% insight, 20% invitation.

Teach something useful. Explain the benefits. Answer FAQ. Share examples. Address objections. Give perspective. Show them the "what" and the "why," give them a peek at the "how," and invite them to connect for the rest of the "how." In many cases, people sell the "how" as their service or product. Then invite the next step. A consultation or first purchase.

People don't want advertising. They want answers. And when your answers are valuable enough, they become your advertising.

Step Six: Now You're Ready for the Engine

By this step, you're no longer guessing.

You have:

- A core message
- A long-form asset
- A library of content
- A destination
- A follow-up sequence

You're ready to run the engine!

Pro Tip (Don't Skip This)

If writing a sales letter or presentation feels overwhelming, here's an easy way in:

Write down:

- 10 frequently asked questions
- 10 "should ask" questions

"Should ask" questions are the ones your clients don't even know to ask yet. Answer those, and you've already started building your entire system.

Now, if you look closely at what we just did, you may start to notice something. We started running a system. A system where each piece of content has a role.

And when I stepped back and looked at this pattern...

Your Step	What It Actually Is
Write sales letter	T — Teach
Long-form video	T — Teach

Chop into clips	A — Attract
"Put 'em in the box"	O — Opportunity
Follow-up sequence	C + I — Curate + Interact
Case studies	N — Network

I realized something. There are really only a handful of things your content ever needs to do. When you understand these, you stop guessing what to create, and you start compounding what you create.

I call this...

The A.C.T.I.O.N. Flywheel

The A.C.T.I.O.N. Flywheel is a cycle you run over and over again rather than a checklist you complete. Each pass builds more momentum than the last. Previously in this chapter, you built a foundation once. Now the flywheel keeps the engine running.

To illustrate its simplicity, there are essentially only six forms of content you need. Just six forms of expression in the world. And when you cycle through these six things, it starts building upon itself, and that's why I call it the A.C.T.I.O.N. Flywheel, and we'll explore it letter by letter. Not only is each letter a category of content, but it's also its priority. You'll create the most in **A**, less in **C**, less in **T**, and so on. It's weighted, strategic, and it works.

Let's go...

A — Attraction Content

Nothing starts without relevant attention. The kind that makes the right person stop and think: *"That's exactly what I've been dealing with."* Attraction content is anything that would make a stranger stop, pay attention, and recognize themselves in what you're saying.

You'll spend most of your time on Attraction content because this is what hooks new eyes on your universe (and draws them to your foundational content). To further clarify, using "feeds" on social platforms is your opportunity to hook new eyes on your foundational content, which is why much of your content should be attraction and discovery content.

Here are some examples:

Problem-Based Hooks

- *"Why your content isn't getting clients (and what to fix instead)"*
- *"The real reason you're not known for anything (yet)"*
- *"Why saving money still doesn't feel like you're getting ahead"*
- *"Why you're working out… but not seeing results"*
- *"What most people don't understand before signing a contract"*

FAQ Content (obvious questions)

- *"What should I actually talk about in my content?"*
- *"Do I need to be on every platform?"*
- *"How much should I really be saving each month?"*
- *"Do I need a lawyer for this situation?"*
- *"What's the best workout plan for beginners?"*

"Should Ask" Questions (hidden problems)

- *"Why your content isn't compounding (even if you're consistent)"*
- *"What most people misunderstand about being consistent"*
- *"Why high earners still feel broke"*
- *"The mistake that turns small disputes into expensive lawsuits"*
- *"Why consistency alone isn't enough to get in shape"*

Relatable Observations

- *"Ever feel like you're posting... but nothing is happening?"*
- *"You're showing up... but not getting known"*
- *"You're making good money... but it still feels tight"*
- *"You thought this would be simple... but it's not"*

Contrarian Takes

- *"Consistency is not your problem"*
- *"Stop trying to go viral"*
- *"Saving more isn't always the solution"*
- *"More workouts won't fix this"*
- *"The legal system doesn't work the way you think it does"*

Quick Wins / Micro-Teaching Hooks

- *"One simple way to make your content instantly clearer"*
- *"How to turn one idea into 10 pieces of content"*
- *"One small money move that can change your future"*
- *"A simple tweak to get more out of every workout"*
- *"One question to ask before signing anything"*

C — Curate & Comment

You don't have to invent every idea. In fact, you shouldn't. Some of the most powerful content is built on ideas that already exist. This will get you more eyeballs than any other kind of content because you are tapping into what revered copywriter Robert Collier said: *"Always enter the conversation already taking place in the customer's mind."* This is why "C" is listed in the higher weight of distribution, just like "A."

Ever notice that some people make their entire career simply commenting on other people's comments? Entire TV shows like TMZ, Extra, or any tabloid TV covering the news of the day are based on interpretation! Remember, be the **interpreter.** You add your perspective. Your judgment. Your standards. You take something familiar and make it yours. You gain more authority because YOU have something to say about it!

T — Teach

This is where your authority starts to stick. You take what you know, and you make it usable, clear, and actionable. Just enough for someone to think: *"That actually helped me."* Because when people learn from you, they begin to trust you. And trust compounds faster than attention ever will.

You're not trying to teach everything. You're trying to teach just enough for someone to make progress. Most experts lose people by over-explaining. One clear takeaway will always outperform ten confusing ones.

Long-form content pays off. One idea chopped up turns into many lessons. And those lessons stack trust.

Here are some examples to get the juices flowing...

Simple How-Tos (immediate value)

- *"How to turn one idea into 5 pieces of content"*
- *"How to explain what you do in one sentence"*
- *"How to reduce your monthly expenses without feeling restricted"* (financial advisor)
- *"How to avoid common contract mistakes before signing"* (lawyer)
- *"How to get more out of a 30-minute workout"* (fitness)

Step-by-Step Breakdowns

- *"3 steps to make your content instantly clearer"*
- *"A simple framework for organizing your ideas"*
- *"3 steps to start building an emergency fund"*
- *"A simple process to prepare for your first legal consultation"*
- *"A 3-step routine to stay consistent with your workouts"*

Clarifying Concepts (make complex simple)

- *"The difference between posting and positioning"*
- *"Why most content doesn't compound"*
- *"The difference between saving and investing"*
- *"What a contract actually protects (and what it doesn't)"*
- *"Why intensity matters more than duration in workouts"*

Mistake Corrections

- *"The biggest mistake people make when creating content"*
- *"What most people get wrong about building authority"*
- *"The mistake that keeps people stuck financially"*

- *"The legal mistake that costs more later"*
- *"Why doing more workouts isn't getting you results"*

Frameworks & Shortcuts

- *"A simple way to decide what to post every day"*
- *"A quick formula for writing better hooks"*
- *"A simple budgeting method that actually works"*
- *"A quick checklist before signing any agreement"*
- *"A simple structure for planning your weekly workouts"*

"Do This, Not That"

- *"Do this instead of trying to go viral"*
- *"Stop doing this if you want your content to work"*
- *"Do this before investing your money"*
- *"Ask this before hiring a lawyer"*
- *"Do this instead of spending hours in the gym"*

Notice the difference? Attraction makes someone stop. Teaching gives them a reason to stay. ***"Put 'em in the box!"***

I — Interactive

Your content stops being one-way and starts becoming a conversation. Interacting with the market shows you're real and not hiding behind an online persona.

Interactive content is any content that invites engagement, such as a question, survey, or poll. It's hard for people to resist when you ask for an opinion! When people engage with your content, the more invested they become.

Keep your questions simple and irresistible:

Simple Questions

- *"Have you experienced this?"*
- *"Does this sound familiar?"*
- *"What's been your biggest struggle with _____?"*

Either / Or Prompts

- *"Clarity or consistency—which do you struggle with more?"*
- *"Save more or invest more—where are you right now?"*
- *"Cardio or strength—what do you default to?"*

Fill-in-the-Blank

- *"The hardest part about content for me is _____"*
- *"I wish I understood this sooner: _____"*

Opinion / Perspective

- *"Do you agree or disagree?"*
- *"What's your take on this?"*

Reflection Prompts

- *"Think about this for a second..."*
- *"Be honest—are you doing this?"*

Comment Triggers (light CTA)

- *"Comment 'PLAN,' and I'll send you something"*
- *"Drop 'HELP' if you want a breakdown"*

Don't just talk to your market, involve them! Interaction creates involvement. But involvement, by itself, doesn't create outcomes. At some point, the conversation has to go somewhere. That's where most people stop short, but that's where opportunity begins.

This is also where comment prompts start to matter more than they seem. When someone comments *"yes," "help,"* or *"interested,"* they're raising their hand. A perfect time to invite them to connect. ***"Put 'em in the box!"***

O — Opportunity

Opportunity content turns trust into next steps without feeling pushy. It shouldn't feel like selling, it should feel like opening a door. Nobody likes content that is mostly "hire me!" That's why it's lower on the distribution weighting.

Here are some examples of how you can tactfully show people what it could be like to work with you. The idea is that you create a piece of content or a video that offers your solution, giving a brief summary or visual. For example, if you're offering your book in your video, you'd hold it up and list the juiciest 3 things they'll get when they download it for free or purchase it for a nominal price. Let's look at a few other example hooks you can riff off of...

Example Soft Invitations

- *"If you struggle with ____, I break this down deeper in my book"*
- *"If you want____, I've got a full training on it"*
- *"If you want help building a plan for ____, I can show you how"*
- *"If you're dealing with _____, it's worth having a conversation"*

- *"If you want a structured approach to____, I've got something for you"*

Resource-Based Invites

- *"Download this checklist before you make a move"*
- *"I created something to help you apply this immediately"*
- *"Grab this budgeting template to get started"*
- *"Use this checklist before signing anything"*
- *"Download this workout plan to stay consistent"*

Conversation Invites

- *"If you want to talk through your situation, let's connect"*
- *"Happy to walk through this with you"*
- *"Let's map this out together"*
- *"If you're not sure what to do next financially, let's talk"*
- *"If you need clarity on your situation, I can help you think it through"*

Authority-Based Invites (show them high-level, then invite)

- "This is exactly what I help clients do"
- "This is something I walk people through every day"
- "This is where I spend most of my time with clients"

These subtly say, *"I do this professionally."*

End Content with an Appropriate Call to Action

- *"Download my book here"*
- *"If you want help with this, here's the next step"*

- *"Book a call if you're ready"*
- *"If this helped, the next step is applying it"*
- *"This is where most people get stuck… and where I can help"*
- *"Knowing this is one thing—implementing it is another"*

Turn every interaction into an opportunity!

N — Network

Network content is the multiplier. The market sees your world, not just what you say, but who surrounds you: your clients, collaborators, mentors, and peers. When you bring others into your content, you're showing association, alignment, and proof. This signals your lineage, your standards, and your place in the market.

Here are some ideas for network content:

- Client case studies and testimonials
- Referral partner interviews
- Interviews with mentors, peers, and industry leaders
- Virtual summits
- Roundtables

People will always evaluate who you are connected to.

HOW YOU BECOME "KNOWN-FOR"

Most people create content randomly. But when you understand A.C.T.I.O.N., everything you create has a role, and you're not guessing anymore. And over time, you gain recognition, authority, and opportunity.

I've seen people go from staring at a blank screen, wondering what to post, to having more ideas than they know what to do with because they finally had a structure that unlocks creativity. A.C.T.I.O.N. is something you operate, not just move through once. You cycle through it again and again like a flywheel.

People don't remember everything you say. They remember what you consistently circulate. When your content is random, nothing sticks. When your content is structured, everything compounds. This is how the gap closes. The gap between **what you know and what you're known for.** Once that gap closes, opportunities start finding you. Conversations become easier. Decisions happen faster. All because your ideas were seen, heard, and remembered again and again. You become **The Navigator.**

You now have the engine. You know how to create, circulate, and compound your ideas. But what if there was one asset that made everything else easier, faster, or unnecessary? In the next chapter, you'll discover the power of authorship and how your Signature Authority Book is the ultimate cashflow content machine. Because you don't need more content. You need an **apex asset.**

KEY TAKEAWAYS

- Stop chasing platforms and start building assets. Algorithms come and go, but strong ideas, clear messaging, and foundational content keep working long after you hit publish.

- Every piece of content needs a job. Attention. Trust. Engagement. Action. Reach. When content has no role, it becomes noise instead of momentum.

- The smartest way to create content is to build once, then multiply. Start with the core message, turn it into a long-form asset, break it into smaller pieces, and direct everything toward one clear next step.

- A.C.T.I.O.N. gives your content structure: **A**ttract, **C**urate, **T**each, **I**nteract, create **O**pportunity, and leverage your **N**etwork. When you cycle through those on purpose, content starts compounding instead of disappearing.

- You do not become known for everything you know. You become known for what your content consistently carries forward, repeats, and reinforces.

CHAPTER

THE APEX ASSET

A Signature Authority Book Turns Your Magic Into What You're "Known-For"

....

"Content is the spark. Social media is the gasoline.
Your book is the fire people gather around."

—MARK IMPERIAL

....

Great news! You're officially **not** thinking like everyone else anymore! You've stopped chasing content and started focusing on what your content is actually *supposed to do.* You've learned how to:

- Recognize your magic
- Articulate your thinking
- Turn your answers into assets
- And deploy those ideas so they circulate

That alone puts you ahead of the vast majority of professionals. But there's still a problem. And if you've felt it, you're not crazy. Even with all that, something is missing. You can have great ideas, create consistent content, and get attention. But without a center, a nucleus, everything you create stays scattered. People encounter pieces of your thinking but never fully understand you.

Content, by itself, is not designed to carry your full message. It's designed to spark curiosity. Curiosity needs somewhere to go. When your content does its job, the right people resonate with it and give you their attention. Not just attention, but *interest* and perhaps, *intent*. They want more of *you*.

So, where do they go?

Right now, most professionals skip the most obvious, most effective, most logical asset of authoring a book (likely due to false beliefs such as "I'm not good enough" or "It must take too much work and time"). Instead, they do more random things. A post here. A video there. A podcast somewhere else. People get in, but they don't really know where they are.

Every brick-and-mortar business has a front door. It's where people enter and immediately understand what they've stepped into. It's decorated intentionally for this very purpose. Now imagine someone trying to enter through the side door. They walk through a messy kitchen. A cluttered hallway. A chaotic back room. That's what random content feels like. Most professionals are sending people through side doors full of out-of-order ideas. And they wonder why people don't fully "get it."

Your book is your "front door." The most intentional, organized, and complete way to enter your world. It's where people finally understand you, gain trust in you, and decide. And once you see it this way, you realize you need something that makes all of your content work; a vessel that holds and compounds your thinking, and gives it a place to land. You need an apex asset. **There is no stronger container and vehicle for your ideas than a book.**

Your Signature Authority Book is how you turn what you know into what you're known for. Your content introduces you. Your book defines you. And this is how you close the Known-For Gap.

I'm sure you've spent time perfecting your presentation. (If not, maybe writing your book will finally force you to do the work you know you've been avoiding?) When you turn your presentation into a book, you create the ultimate, non-salesy salesperson. It delivers your message perfectly. Every time. It never forgets. It never gets tired. It never calls in sick.

And if you want more "perfect salespeople"? Print more copies. The power of a book allows you to build authority and nurture new prospects at scale.

THE ONE THING

In his bestselling book "The ONE Thing," author Gary Keller (with Jay Papasan) poses a deceptively simple question that has become a cornerstone of modern productivity thinking:

"What's the ONE thing I can do such that by doing it, everything else will be easier or unnecessary?"

This powerful question challenges you to identify the single most important action that drives meaningful results and clarity in your work and life. Right now, for your business, that ONE thing is having a Signature Authority Book.

> → Marketing = BETTER & EASIER
> → Sales = BETTER & EASIER (arguably UNNECESSARY)
> → Prospecting = BETTER & EASIER
> → Attracting Media Opportunities (TV, Radio, Podcast, Stage) = BETTER & EASIER or UNNECESSARY
> → Long Nurturing Conversations = UNNECESSARY
> → Convincing Someone You're the Expert = UNNECESSARY

THE APEX ASSET DECISION

A book finally gives your ideas a place to live outside of you. You already have the thinking. You already have the experience. You already have the answers people are looking for. The only question is: Will you document it, or let it stay invisible? If you don't capture your thinking, you can't be known for it.

Some people hesitate because they think this is a massive project. Others hesitate because they think they're not writers. And many suffer from imposter syndrome: *"Who am I to have a book?"* **Everyone who believes in being an educator and an advocate for their clients' success deserves a book.**

At a certain level, not having a book is the bottleneck. The missing thing that forces you to keep explaining yourself over and over again while you stay virtually unknown. And if you're someone who doesn't want the spotlight, when you have a book, you're good because if you don't want to do the talking, your book will do it for you! Not everyone wants to be on stage, be interviewed, or always be "on." That's totally fine, but your message still needs to move.

A book upgrades everything about your business and how you operate. Your marketing becomes clearer. Your sales become easier. Suddenly, your clients are better. They pay more (and happily), because they're informed and they know how to show up.

A business without a book is like a house or a car without air conditioning. You could live without it, but why would you?

A BOOK TRANSCENDS TIME

Another huge, overlooked benefit of a book is that it transcends time. When I speak or sponsor an event, the conference is a giant ball of over-stimulation for attendees. They want more from you, but they have limited time, and they don't want to miss anything. What they do is "mentally shortlist" what is important for them to remember and "check out when I get home." The problem is, what are you giving them to "check out?" A brochure? A business card? A pen?

When I speak on stage or meet people at my trade show booth, they get to "take me with them" through my book. Think about it: I lit a fire in them about my topic, and for the people who make it a priority, my book is the ultimate engagement device! Because now I'm on their shortlist. I didn't give them a salesy brochure or some meaningless tchotchke like a pen or a keychain; I gave them a resource. They can immerse themselves in my thinking for HOURS, happily, and I won't have to be there. Maybe *you're* doing that right now? *smile*

Google's 7-11-4 research study showed that, on average, for people to have enough information to decide if they will do business with you, they need an average of seven hours of "immersion" with you through 11 different touchpoints (emails, articles, videos, etc.) in an average of four different settings (writings, videos, in-person, etc.) A book is a <u>great</u> way to get those hours in!

THE SIMPLEST PATH FORWARD

At this point, the question isn't *if* this makes sense. It's how to actually do it without overcomplicating it. You don't have to spend months or years trying to find the perfect words and how to say them. Most people get stuck staring at a blank page and stay stuck.

There's a better way…

Your Book Done in 90 Days or Less… Without AI and No Writing Needed

The good news is, this is not what most people think it is. You don't have to sit down for months in isolation, racking your brain, trying to crank out a manuscript. If you're open to it, I can show you a streamlined path. The same system my team and I have helped over 800+ clients dominate their fields with since 2008, and it's only four phases:

1. We memorialize your magic (what you already know and should be known for).
2. We interview your thinking (so you can speak naturally instead of writing).

3. We write (humans, no AI), design, and publish for your approval, turning your ideas into a world-class asset.

4. You enjoy better clients, faster…<u>forever</u> (because people finally understand you before they ever meet you).

That's it.

I've helped hundreds of professionals do this over nearly two decades, and I've seen what happens when they finally make the decision. They establish their authority in their market, even if they've been invisible for years. They fill their pipelines faster and easier than ever before. And they gain better, premium clients that value them in record time. Which is why, at this point, not offering to help you would feel like malpractice.

I've seen too many people fail because they:

- Put this off for years
- Try to write the hard, frustrating way that never gets finished
- Write the wrong book for the wrong audience or for the wrong reason
- Or never do it at all

And I don't want that to happen to you. How much money have you lost by *not* having a book? A year from now, will your book be out there landing better, higher-paying clients and easier wins, or still sitting half-done?

So here's what I'd recommend. If this is clicking for you… let's talk. **Go to: ☞ www.booksgrowbusiness.com**

Schedule a complimentary **Bookstorming Session**. We'll take about 20–30 minutes. I'll learn about your work, your goals, and what you want to be known for. And if a book makes sense, I'll show you exactly what it should be, and the smartest way to make it real. No pressure and no obligation. You can take my ideas and run with them either way.

Seth Godin said, *"The book that will change your life the most is the one you write,"* and it couldn't be more true. Writing forces you to decide, to define, and to declare. It turns scattered experience into clear doctrine and makes your thinking transferable to the people who need it most. This is how you turn **what you know into what you're known for.**

KEY TAKEAWAYS

- Content sparks interest, but without a central asset, your message never fully comes together.

- A book is your front door, the place where people finally understand you, trust you, and decide.

- When one asset makes marketing clearer, sales easier, and positioning obvious, it stops being optional and becomes the move.

- If your thinking isn't captured, it can't compound, and if it doesn't compound, you stay explaining instead of being known.

- A book turns your ideas into doctrine, and what you know into what you're known for.

THE BUSINESS OWNER CREATOR

A New Class of Entrepreneurs

> "You're not here just to create content.
> You're here to become known for something."
>
> —MARK IMPERIAL

If you've read this far and really taken it in, you're not the same business owner you were when you started. You now see why your expertise wasn't turning into authority, why others became known while you stayed in the background, and why content often felt confusing or pointless.

More importantly, you now know what to do next. You have the model, the language, and the system. If you use what you've learned, people in your market won't be able to ignore you. You'll build real assets and be known for something.

HERE'S WHO YOU'VE BECOME...

You're now a **Business Owner Creator.** This new identity means you think, act, and succeed in a different way.

THE BUSINESS OWNER CREATOR MANIFESTO
The Credo of Those Who Refuse to Stay Unknown

I. THE REALIZATION

Experts didn't lose value. The market lost the ability to see it. Great ideas were never written down. Important thoughts stayed stuck in conversations. Answers vanished as soon as they were spoken. When expertise stays hidden, so does your business.

II. THE PROBLEM: THE KNOWN-FOR GAP

There is a gap between what you know and what the market knows you for. That gap is where you lose opportunities. The market rewards ideas that are easy to find, share, and understand. If your ideas don't get out there, you won't grow.

III. THE SHIFT

We are here to build real assets, not just make more content.
Content is temporary. Assets are permanent.
Content creates motion. Assets create momentum.

IV. THE TRUTH

You are not known for what you know...
You are known for what people can access.
If your ideas aren't documented, they don't exist in the market.

V. THE APEX PRINCIPLE

There is one asset that changes everything. The one place where your thinking is:

- organized
- complete
- undeniable

Your Signature Authority Book. It becomes the core of your business.

VI. THE IDENTITY

We are Business Owner Creators.
We write things down, teach, stand up for our ideas, and publish our work. We focus on what matters. We build systems that do the explaining for us so we don't have to repeat ourselves.

VII. THE ADVANTAGE

Content helps people notice you. A book helps people choose you. Without a book, your ideas just move around. With a book, they grow and build on each other. Your expertise alone can't reach more people. But when you write down your ideas, they can.

VIII. THE STANDARD

Clarity over noise. Answers over advertising. Authority over attention. Structure over randomness. We don't post just to keep busy. We publish so people know who we are.

IX. THE PROMISE

We will no longer let our best ideas disappear. We won't stay invisible while less qualified voices get all the attention. We won't leave it up to luck for people to understand us. We will document our ideas. We will be known for something that resonates with our audience.

X. THE CALL

This is the era of the Business Owner Creator.
Your ideas transform into assets, your expertise becomes authority, and your content produces predictable cashflow.

**This is how you turn what you know
into what you're known for.**

— Mark Imperial
Founder of ActionBrand™
Author, Cashflow Content

WILL YOU ANSWER THE CALL?

Business Owner Creator is a movement. Movements need three things: standards, a shared language, and **people who see what you see.** That's why we created this:

THE BUSINESS OWNER CREATORS ASSOCIATION

This is more than a networking group, content community, or another place to simply learn. As a member, you get tools to build your authority, access ongoing support from peers and experts, and opportunities to grow your audience and impact.

People like you come together to **become known for something that matters, to build real assets, and to compound their thinking into authority, opportunity, and cashflow.**

If this book spoke to you, if you saw yourself in these pages, if you've ever felt overlooked, or if you've known you had more to offer than people realized,

You already belong here.

BUSINESS OWNER CREATORS ASSOCIATION

☞ **Step Into the Business Owner Creators Association**

www.BusinessOwnerCreators.org

This is your moment.

Not to start creating more content, **but to finally become known for your magic.**

ABOUT MARK IMPERIAL

Mark Imperial is the architect behind a new class of entrepreneurs: **Business Owner Creators.** A movement built on a simple but powerful idea: What you know should be working for you long after you say it.

For over two decades, Mark has been obsessed with one question: *"Why do some experts become known for something while others, just as talented, remain invisible?"* That question led him to develop a body of work that bridges branding, direct response marketing, and authorship into one unified system for turning ideas into assets. He calls it **ActionBrand**™, which is a philosophy built on a contrarian truth: You don't build a brand to get a customer. You get a customer to build a brand.

Before creating this framework, Mark trained under legendary marketer Dan S. Kennedy and became one of his Certified Independent Business Advisors. He went on to lead Kennedy's Chicago Mastermind Group for eight years and contributed to the *No B.S. Marketing Letter*, influencing tens of thousands of business owners.

At the same time, Mark was in the field implementing marketing for globally recognized brands, including Nintendo™, Pokémon™, and Under Armour™, where he saw firsthand how attention is captured and, more importantly, sustained.

However, it wasn't until he began helping professionals turn their expertise into books that something clicked. The real asset wasn't content. It was documented thinking. That realization led to the creation of his three-part body of work:

- *ActionBrand Marketing* — the system for building a brand that converts
- *Cashflow Content* — the engine for turning ideas into authority and income
- *Books Grow Business* — the apex asset that anchors it all

Together, they form a complete model for becoming known for something in a world drowning in noise.

Mark has since directly helped nearly 1,000 business owners, advisors, and experts transform what they know into marketable, memorable intellectual property, positioning them as the go-to authority in their field. In today's economy, the people who win are not the ones who know the most. They are the ones who become known for something specific.

Mark lives in the western suburbs of Chicago with his beloved Shannon, and their precocious pug pup brothers, Gordon Whitefoot and Humphrey Pugfart. Yes, those are their real names. And yes, they were named that way on purpose. Because even in a house full of dogs, what gets named right gets remembered.

WHAT MARK'S CLIENTS ARE SAYING...

"The best marketing tool you can create, quite honestly, is a book. It established credibility and allowed us to communicate our services to clients and prospects in a non-intrusive way, facilitating conversations and introductions. The book was the best marketing decision we've made.

I had thought about writing a book for years, but saw it as a monumental hurdle. I didn't know if I had the time or if I could do it. After meeting Mark, we discussed the process and timeline. His approach was efficient and streamlined. Mark broke it down into manageable chunks I felt I could handle. I was excited about the timeline and how it could help us scale our business and serve as a resource to our clients about what we do and how we can help.

We've already signed on several new clients, and it's helped us clarify our process. This is something I would've never thought we could do, until we had met Mark and his team, quite honestly. I'm more than thrilled with the experience and the outcome."

Jayne McQuillan CPA, MBA, CEPA
Best-Selling Author, The Value Journey
www.journeyconsult.com/the-value-journey-book

"I wanted to write a book to get my message out so that it will live beyond me, beyond my retirement. I had so much sitting in my head, and I didn't know how to fit it all into a book.

Part of the reason I didn't want to start was that it just sounded overwhelming. I didn't know where to begin. Mark coached me on how to say it and simplify it so it's easy to remember and becomes true intellectual property.

He who owns the name owns the intellectual property. So I'm very, very grateful to Mark for helping me. Mark packaged all those systems and my ideas, making it so much easier to communicate. I love that he and Shannon have a system. They really did an excellent job of breaking down the outline, so I only needed to think about one chapter at a time. When I have a conversation with a prospect, honestly, it's hard to articulate 20+ years of experience within 10 minutes. So now I start with 'Hey, why don't I mail you my book?' Just the fact that I can tell people I published a book and it was an Amazon bestseller gives me instant credibility. I have a new identity now, I'm an author, and instantly people say, 'Wow!'

If you are a professional or business owner and want to touch more lives or be bigger than who you are now, definitely consider writing a book."

Violetta Terpeluk MBA, CFP, CEPA
Best-Selling Author, Financial Flow
www.financialflowbook.com

"*I'd always considered writing a book. I had no idea where to start. It just seemed overwhelming. Mark put the pieces of the puzzle together for me, and we made it work. His process was seamless. It was easy. It drew out what I already knew and put it into a comprehensive, understandable format. Mark just made the process easy. It was delightful. He understands where I'm coming from, how busy I am, and he led me through the process step by step.*

We got results from the book before it was even done, just by talking about it and putting it out there. It builds credibility and leads to more business. You can hand someone the book and say, 'Go to Chapter Three,' and it becomes something you can refer to.

It's been exciting and fun. Becoming a published author on Amazon and being able to point to my book is pretty cool!"

Rod Chamberlin
Best-Selling Author, Beyond Exit Planning
www.beyondexitplanning.com